THEY WHO KNOCK AT OUR GATES

A COMPLETE
GOSPEL OF IMMIGRATION

BY

MARY ANTIN

WITH ILLUSTRATIONS BY
JOSEPH STELLA

First published in 1914

This edition published by Read Books Ltd.
Copyright © 2017 Read Books Ltd.
This book is copyright and may not be
reproduced or copied in any way without
the express permission of the publisher in writing

British Library Cataloguing-in-Publication Data
A catalogue record for this book is available
from the British Library

THE SINEW AND BONE OF ALL THE NATIONS

CONTENTS

THE MAKING OF A PATRIOT: MARY ANTIN.........7
INTRODUCTION....................................21
THE LAW OF THE FATHERS........................23
JUDGES IN THE GATE.............................36
THE FIERY FURNACE..............................66

THE MAKING OF A PATRIOT: MARY ANTIN

From
Heroines of Service by Mary Lyon
Published In 1921

Where is the true man's fatherland?
Is it where he by chance is born?
Doth not the yearning spirit scorn
In such scant borders to be spanned?
O yes! his fatherland must be
As the blue heaven wide and free!

James Russell Lowell.

THE MAKING OF A PATRIOT

YOU know the story of "The Man without a Country"—the man who lost his country through his own fault. Can you imagine what it would mean to be a child without a country—to have no flag, no heroes, no true native land to which you belong as you belong to your family, and which in turn belongs to you? How would it seem to grow up without the feeling that you have a big country, a true fatherland to protect your home and your friends; to build schools for you; to give you parks and playgrounds, and clean, beautiful streets; to fight disease and many dangers on land and water for you?—This is the story of a little girl who was born in a land where she had no chance for "life, liberty, and the pursuit of happiness." Far from being a true fatherland, her country was like the cruel stepmother of the old tales.

It was strange that one could be born in a country and yet have no right to live there! Little Maryashe (or Mashke, as she was called, because she was too tiny a girl for a big-sounding name) soon learned that the Russia where she was born was not her own country. It seemed that the Russians did not love her people, or want them to live in their big land. And yet there they were! Truly it was a strange world.

"Why is Father afraid of the police?" asked little Mashke. "He has done nothing wrong."

"My child, the trouble is that we can do nothing right!" cried her mother, wringing her hands. "Everything is wrong with us. We have no rights, nothing that we dare to call our own."

It seemed that Mashke's people had to live in a special part of the country called the "Pale of Settlement." It was against the law to go outside the Pale no matter how hard it was to make a living where many people of the same manner of life were herded together, no matter how much you longed to try your fortune in a new place. It was not a free land, this Polotzk where she had been born. It was a prison with iron laws that shut people away from any chance for happy living.

It is hard to live in a cage, be it large or small. Like a wild bird, the free human spirit beats its wings against any bars.

"Why, Mother, why is it that we must not go outside the Pale?" asked Mashke.

"Because the Czar and those others who have the power to make the laws do not love our people; they hate us and all our ways," was the reply.

"But why do they hate us, Mother?" persisted the child with big, earnest eyes.

"Because we are different; because we can never think like them and be like them. Their big Russia is not yet big enough to give people of another sort a chance to live and be happy in their own way."

Even in crowded Polotzk, though, with police spying on every side, there were happy days. There were the beautiful Friday afternoons when Mashke's father and mother came home early from the store to put off every sign of the work-a-day world and make ready for the Sabbath. The children were allowed to wear their holiday clothes and new shoes. They stepped about happily while their mother hid the great store keys and the money bag under her featherbed, and the grandmother sealed the oven and cleared every trace of work from the kitchen.

How Mashke loved the time of candle prayer! As she looked at the pure flame of her candle the light shone in her face and in her heart. Then she looked at the work-worn faces of her mother and grandmother. All the lines of care and trouble were smoothed away in the soft light. They had escaped from the prison of this unfriendly land with its hard laws and its hateful Pale. They were living in the dim but glorious Past, when their father's fathers had been a free nation in a land of their own.

But Mashke could not escape from the prison in that way. She was young and glad to be alive. Her candle shone for light and life to-day and to-morrow and to-morrow! There were no bars that could shut away her free spirit from the light.

How glad she was for life and sunlight on the peaceful Sabbath afternoons when, holding to her father's hand, she walked beyond the city streets along the riverside to the place where in blossoming orchards birds sang of the joyful life of the air, and where in newly plowed fields peasants sang the song of planting-time and the fruitful earth. Her heart leaped as she felt herself a part of the life that flowed through all things—river, air, earth, trees, birds, and happy, toiling people.

It seemed to Mashke that most of her days were passed in wondering—wondering about the strange world in which she found herself, and its strange ways. Of course she played as the children about her did, with her rag doll and her "jacks" made of the knuckle bones of sheep; and she learned to dance to the most spirited tune that could be coaxed from the teeth of a comb covered with a bit of paper. In winter she loved to climb in the bare sledge, which when not actively engaged in hauling wood could give a wonderful joy-ride to a party of happy youngsters, who cared nothing that their sleigh boasted only straw and burlap in place of cushions and fur robes, and a knotted rope in place of reins with jingling bells.

But always, winter and summer, in season and out of season, Mashke found herself wondering about the meaning of all the things that she saw and heard. She wondered about her hens who gave her eggs and broth, and feathers for her bed, all in exchange for her careless largess of grain. Did they ever feel that the barnyard was a prison? She wondered about the treadmill horse who went round and round to pump water for the public baths. Did he know that he was cheated out of the true life of a horse— work-time in cheerful partnership with man and play-time in the pasture with the fresh turf under his road-weary hoofs? Did the women, who toiled over the selfsame tasks in such a weary round that they looked forward to the change of wash-day at the river where they stood knee-deep in the water to rub and scrub their poor rags, know that they, too, were in a treadmill?—Sometimes she could not sleep for wondering, and would steal from her bed before daybreak to walk through the dewy grass of the yard and watch the blackness turn to soft, dreamy gray. Then the houses seemed like breathing creatures, and all the world was hushed and very sweet. Was there ever such a wonder as the coming of a new day?—As she watched it seemed that her spirit flew beyond the town, beyond the river and the glowing sky itself—touching, knowing, and loving all things. Her spirit was free!

Sometimes it seemed that the wings of her spirit could all but carry her little body up and away. She was indeed such a wee mite that they sometimes called her Mouse and Crumb and Poppy Seed. All of her eager, flaming life was in her questioning eyes and her dark, wayward curls. Because she was small and frail she was spared the hard work that early fell to the lot of her older, stronger sister. So it happened that she had time for her wonderings—time for her spirit to grow and try its wings.

Mashke was still a very little child when she learned a very big truth. She discovered that there were many prisons besides those made by Russian laws; she saw that her people often shut themselves up in prisons of their own making. There were hundreds of laws and observances—ways to wash, to eat, to dress, to work—which seemed to many as sacred as their faith in God. Doubtless the rules which were now only empty forms had once had meaning, such as the law forbidding her people to touch fire on the Sabbath, which came down from a time before matches or tinder-boxes when making a fire was hard work. But all good people observed the letter of the law, and, no matter what the need of mending a fire or a light, would wait for a Gentile helper to come to the rescue.

One memorable evening, however, Mashke saw her father, when he thought himself unobserved, quietly steal over to the table and turn down a troublesome lamp. The gleam of a new light came to the mind of the watching, wondering child at that moment. She began to understand that even her father, who was the wisest man in Polotzk, did many things because he feared to offend the prejudices of their people, just as he did many other things because of fear of the Russian police. There was more than one kind of a prison.

When Mashke was about ten years old a great change came to her life. Her father decided to go on a long journey to a place far from Polotzk and its rules of life, far from Russia and its laws of persecution and death, to a true Promised Land where all people, it was said, no matter what their nation and belief, were free to live and be happy in their own way. The name of this Promised Land was America. Some friendly people—the "emigration society," her father called them—made it possible for him to go try his fortune in the new country. Soon he would make a home there for them all.

At last the wonderful letter came—a long letter, and yet it

could not tell the half of his joy in the Promised Land. He had not found riches—no, he had been obliged to borrow the money for the third-class tickets he was sending them—but he had found freedom. Best of all, his children might have the chance to go to school and learn the things that make a free life possible and worth while.

Mashke found that they had suddenly become the most important people in Polotzk. All the neighbors gathered about to see the marvelous tickets that could take a family across the sea. Cousins who had not thought of them for months came with gifts and pleadings for letters from the new world. "Do not forget us when you are so happy and grand," they said.

"You will see my boy, my Möshele," cried a poor mother again and again. "Ask him why he does not write to us these many months. If you do not find him in Boston maybe he will be in Balti-moreh. It is all America."

The day came at last when every stool and feather-bed was sold, and their clothes and all the poor treasures they could carry were wrapped in queer-looking bundles ready to be taken in their arms to the new home. All of Polotzk went to the station to wave gay handkerchiefs and bits of calico and wish them well. They soon found, however, that the way of the emigrant is hard. In order to reach the sea they had to go through Germany to Hamburg, and a fearful journey it proved to be. It was soon evident that the Russians were not the only cruel people in the world; the Germans were just as cruel in strange and unusual ways, and in a strange language.

They put the travelers in prison, for which they had a queer name, of course—"Quarantine," they called it. They drove them like cattle into a most unpleasant place, where their clothes were snatched off, their bodies rubbed with an evil, slippery substance, and their breath taken away by an unexpected shower that suddenly descended on their helpless heads. Their precious bundles, too, were tossed about rudely and steamed and smoked. As the poor victims sat wrapped in clouds of steam waiting for the final agony, their clothes were brought back, steaming like everything else, and somebody cried, "Quick! Quick! or you will lose your train!" It seemed that they were not to be murdered after all, but that this was just the German way of treating people whom they thought capable of carrying diseases about with them.

Then came the sixteen days on the big ship, when Mashke was too ill part of the time even to think about America. But there were better days, when the coming of morning found her near the rail gazing at the path of light that led across the shimmering waves into the heart of the golden sky. That way seemed like her own road ahead into the new life that awaited her.

The golden path really began at a Boston public school. Here Mashke stood in her new American dress of stiff calico and gave a new American name to the friendly teacher of the primer class. Mary Antin she was called from that day, all superfluous foreign letters being dropped off forever. As her father tried in his broken English to tell the teacher something of his hopes for his children, Mary knew by the look in his eyes that he, too, had a vision of the path of light. The teacher also saw that glowing, consecrated look and in a flash of insight comprehended something of his starved past and the future for which he longed. In his effort to make himself understood he talked with his hands, with his shoulders, with his eyes; beads of perspiration stood out on his earnest brow, and now he dropped back helplessly into Yiddish, now into Russian. "I cannot now learn what the world knows; I must work. But I bring my children—they go to school for me. I am American citizen; I want my children be American citizens."

The first thing was, of course, to make a beginning with the new language. Afterward when Mary Antin was asked to describe the way the teacher had worked with her foreign class she replied with a smile, "I can't vouch for the method, but the six children in my own particular group (ranging in age from six to fifteen—I was then twelve) attacked the see-the-cat and look-at-the-hen pages of our primers with the keenest zest, eager to find how the common world looked, smelled, and tasted in the strange speech, and we learned!" There was a dreadful time over learning to say *the* without making a buzzing sound; even mastering the v's and w's was not so hard as that. It was indeed a proud day for Mary Antin when she could say "We went to the village after water," to her teacher's satisfaction.

How Mary Antin loved the American speech! She had a native gift for language, and gathered the phrases eagerly, lovingly, as one gathers flowers, ever reaching for more and still more. She said the words over and over to herself with shining eyes as the miser counts his gold. Soon she found that she was thinking in the beautiful English way. When she had been only four months at school she wrote a composition on *Snow* that her teacher had printed in a school journal to show this foreign child's wonderful progress in the use of the new tongue. Here is a bit of that composition:

> Now the trees are bare, and no flowers are to see in the fields and gardens (we all know why), and the whole world seems like a-sleep without the happy bird songs which left us till spring. But the snow which drove away all these pretty and happy things, try (as I think) not to make us at all unhappy; they covered up the branches of the trees, the fields, the gardens and houses, and the whole world looks like dressed in a beautiful white—instead of green—dress, with the sky looking down on it with a pale face....

At the middle of the year the child who had entered the primer class in September without a word of English was promoted to the fifth grade. She was indeed a proud girl when she went home with her big geography book making a broad foundation for all the rest of the pile, which she loved to carry back and forth just because it made her happy and proud to be seen in company with books.

"Look at that pale, hollow-chested girl with that load of books," said a kindly passer-by one day. "It is a shame the way children are overworked in school these days."

The child in question, however, would have had no basis for understanding the chance sympathy had she overheard the words. Her books were her dearest joy. They were indeed in a very real sense her only tangible possessions. All else was as yet "the stuff that dreams are made of." As she walked through the dingy, sordid streets her glorified eyes looked past the glimpses of unlovely life about her into a beautiful world of her own. If she felt any weight from the books she carried it was just a comfortable reminder that this new Mary Antin and the new life of glorious opportunity were real.

When she climbed the two flights of stairs to her wretched tenement her soul was not soiled by the dirt and squalor through which she passed. As she eagerly read, not only her school history but also every book she could find in the public library about the heroes of America, she did not see the moldy paper hanging in shreds from the walls or the grimy bricks of the neighboring factory that shut out the sunlight. Her look was for the things beyond the moment—the things that really mattered. How could the child feel poor and deprived when she knew that the city of Boston was hers!

As she walked every afternoon past the fine, dignified buildings and churches that flanked Copley Square to the imposing granite structure that held all her hero books, she walked as a princess into her palace. Could she not read for herself the inscription at the entrance: Public Library—Built by the People—Free to All—? Now she stood and looked about her and said, "This is real. This all belongs to these wide-awake children, these fine women, these learned men—and to *me*."

Every nook of the library that was open to the public became familiar to her; her eyes studied lovingly every painting and bit of mosaic. She spent hours pondering the vivid pictures by Abbey that tell in color the mystic story of Sir Galahad and the quest of the Holy Grail, and it seemed as if the spirit of all romance was hers. She lingered in the gallery before Sargent's pictures of the "Prophets," and it seemed as if the spirit of all the beautiful Sabbaths of her childhood stirred within her, as echoes of the Hebrew psalms awoke in her memory.

When she went into the vast reading-room she always chose a place at the end where, looking up from her books, she could get the effect of the whole vista of splendid arches and earnest readers. It was in the courtyard, however, that she felt the keenest joy. Here the child born in the prison of the Pale realized to the full the glorious freedom that was hers.

"The courtyard was my sky-roofed chamber of dreams," she said. "Slowly strolling past the endless pillars of the colonnade, the fountain murmured in my ear of all the beautiful things in all the beautiful world. Here I liked to remind myself of Polotzk, the better to bring out the wonder of my life. That I who was brought up to my teens almost without a book should be set down in the midst of all the books that ever were written was a miracle as great as any on record. That an outcast should become a privileged citizen, that a beggar should dwell in a palace—this was a romance more thrilling than poet ever sung. Surely I was rocked in an enchanted cradle."

As Mary Antin's afternoons were made glorious by these visits to the public library, so her nights were lightened by rare half-hours on the South Boston Bridge where it crosses the Old Colony Railroad. As she looked down at the maze of tracks and the winking red and green signal lights, her soul leaped at the thought of the complex world in which she lived and the wonderful way in which it was ordered and controlled by the mind of man. Years afterward in telling about her dreams on the bridge she said:

"Then the blackness below me was split by the fiery eye of a monster engine, his breath enveloped me in blinding clouds, his long body shot by, rattling a hundred claws of steel, and he was gone. So would I be, swift on my rightful business, picking out my proper track from the million that cross it, pausing for no obstacles, sure of my goal."

Can you imagine how the child from Polotzk loved the land that had taken her to itself? As she stood up in school with the other children and saluted the Stars and Stripes, the words she said seemed to come from the depths of her soul: "I pledge allegiance to my flag and to the Republic for which it stands—one nation indivisible, with liberty and justice for all." Those were not words, they were heart throbs. The red of the flag was not just a bright color, it was the courage of heroes; the white was the symbol of truth clear as the sunlight; the blue was the symbol of the wide, free heavens—her spirit's fatherland. The child who had been born in prison, who had repeated at every Passover, "Next year, may we be in Jerusalem," had found all at once her true country, her flag, and her heroes. When the children rose to sing "America," she sang with all the pent-up feeling of starved years of exile:

I love thy rocks and rills,
Thy woods and templed hills.

As the teacher looked into the glorified face of this little alien-citizen she said to herself, "There is the truest patriot of them all!"

Only once as they were singing "Land where my fathers died," the child's voice had faltered and died away. Her cheek paled when at the close of school she came to her teacher with her trouble.

"Oh, teacher," she mourned, "our country's song can't to mean me—*my* fathers didn't die here!"

The friendly teacher, whose understanding and sympathy were never failing, understood now:

"Mary Antin," she said earnestly, looking through the child's great, dark eyes into the depths of her troubled soul, "you have as much right to those words as I or anybody else in America. The Pilgrim Fathers didn't all come here before the Revolution. Isn't your father just like them? Think of it, dear, how he left his home and came to a strange land where he couldn't even speak the language. And didn't he come looking for the same things? He wanted freedom for himself and his family, and a chance for his children to grow up wise and brave. It's the same story over again. Every ship that brings people from Russia and other countries where they are ill-treated is a *Mayflower*!"

These words took root in Mary Antin's heart and grew with her growth. The consciousness that she was in very truth an American glorified her days; it meant freedom from every prison. Seven years after her first appearance in the Boston primer class she entered Barnard College. After two years there and two more at Teachers College, she entered the school of life as a homemaker; her name is now Mary Antin Grabau. Besides caring for her home and her little daughter, she has devoted her gifts as a writer and a lecturer to the service of her country.

In her book, "The Promised Land," she has told the story of her life from the earliest memories of her childhood in Russia to the time when she entered college. It is an absorbing human story, but it is much more than that. It is the story of one who looks upon her American citizenship as a great "spiritual adventure," and who strives to quicken in others a sense of their opportunities and responsibilities as heirs of the new freedom. She pleads for a generous treatment of all those whom oppression and privation send to make their homes in our land. It is only by being faithful to the ideal of human brotherhood expressed in the Declaration of Independence that our nation can realize its true destiny, she warns us.

Mary Antin was recently urged to write a history of the United States for children, that would give the inner meaning of the facts as well as a clear account of the really significant events.

> "I have long had such a work in mind," she wrote, "and I suppose I shall have to do it some day. In the meantime I *talk* history to my children—my little daughter of eight and the Russian cousin who goes to school in the kitchen. Only yesterday at luncheon I told them about our system

of representative government, and our potatoes grew cold on our plates, we were all so absorbed."

In all that Mary Antin writes and in all that she says her faith in her country and her zeal for its honor shine out above all else. To the new pilgrims who lived and suffered in other lands before they sought refuge in America, as well as to those who can say quite literally, "Land where my fathers died," she brings this message:

"We must strive to be worthy of our great heritage as American citizens so that we may use wisely and well its wonderful privileges. To be alive in America is to ride on the central current of the river of modern life; and to have a conscious purpose is to hold the rudder that steers the ship of fate."

INTRODUCTION

THREE main questions may be asked with reference to immigration—

First: A question of principle: Have we any right to regulate immigration?

Second: A question of fact: What is the nature of our present immigration?

Third: A question of interpretation: Is immigration good for us?

The difficulty with the first question is to get its existence recognized. In a matter that has such obvious material aspects as the immigration problem the abstract principles involved are likely to be overlooked. But as there can be no sound conclusions without a foundation in underlying principles, this discussion must begin by seeking an answer to the ethical question involved.

The second question is not easy to answer for the reason that men are always poor judges of their contemporaries, especially of those whose interests appear to clash with their own. We suffer here, too, from a bewildering multiplicity of testimony. Every sort of expert whose specialty in any way touches the immigrant has diagnosed the subject according to the formulæ of his own special science—and our doctors disagree! One is forced to give up the luxury of a second-hand opinion on this subject, and to attempt a little investigation of one's own, checking off the dicta of the specialists as well as an amateur may.

The third question, while not wholly separable from the second, is nevertheless an inquiry of another sort. Whether immigration is good for us depends partly on the intrinsic nature of the immigrant and partly on our reactions to his presence. The effects of immigration, produced by the immigrant in partnership with ourselves, some men will approve and some deplore, according to their notions of good and bad. That thing is good for me which leads to my ultimate happiness; and we do not all delight in the same things. The third question, therefore, more than either of the others, each man has to answer for himself.

THEY WHO KNOCK AT OUR GATES

I

THE LAW OF THE FATHERS

And these words, which I command thee this day, shall be in thine heart: and thou shalt teach them diligently unto thy children. . . . And thou shalt write them upon the posts of thy house, and on thy gates.

DEUT. VI, 6, 7, 9.

IF I ask an American what is the fundamental American law, and he does not answer me promptly, "That which is contained in the Declaration of Independence," I put him down for a poor citizen. He who is ignorant of the law is likely to disobey it. And there cannot be two minds about the position of the Declaration among our documents of state. What the Mosaic Law is to the Jews, the Declaration is to the American people. It affords us a starting-point in history and defines our mission among the nations. Without it, we should not differ greatly from other nations who have achieved a constitutional form of government and various democratic institutions. What marks us out from other advanced nations is the origin of our liberties in one supreme act of political innovation, prompted by a conscious sense of the dignity of manhood. In other countries advances have been made by favor of hereditary rulers and aristocratic parliaments, each successive reform being grudgingly handed down to the people from above. Not so in America. At one bold stroke we shattered the monarchical tradition, and installed the people in the seats of government, substituting the gospel of the sovereignty of the masses for the superstition of the divine right of kings.

And even more notable than the boldness of the act was the dignity with which it was entered upon. In terms befitting a philosophical discourse, we gave notice to the world that what we were about to do, we would do in the name of humanity, in the conviction that as justice is the end of government so should manhood be its source.

It is this insistence on the philosophic sanction of our revolt that gives the sublime touch to our political performance. Up to the moment of our declaration of independence, our struggle with our English rulers did not differ from other popular struggles against despotic governments. Again and again we respectfully petitioned for redress of specific grievances, as the governed, from time immemorial, have petitioned their governors. But one day we abandoned our suit for petty damages, and instituted a suit for the recovery of our entire human heritage of freedom; and by basing our claim on the fundamental principles of the brotherhood of man and the sovereignty of the masses, we assumed the championship of the oppressed against their oppressors, wherever found.

It was thus, by sinking our particular quarrel with George of England in the universal quarrel of humanity with injustice, that we emerged a distinct nation, with a unique mission in the world. And we revealed ourselves to the world in the Declaration of Independence, even as the Israelites revealed themselves in the Law of Moses. From the Declaration flows our race consciousness, our sense of what is and what is not American. Our laws, our policies, the successive steps of our progress—all must conform to the spirit of the Declaration of Independence, the source of our national being.

The American confession of faith, therefore, is a recital of the doctrines of liberty and equality. A faithful American is one who understands these doctrines and applies them in his life.

It should be easy to pick out the true Americans—the spiritual heirs of the founders of our Republic—by this simple test of loyalty to the principles of the Declaration. To such a test we are put, both as a nation and as individuals, every time we are asked to define our attitude on immigration. Having set up a government on a declaration of the rights of man, it should be our first business to reaffirm that declaration every time we meet a case involving human rights. Now every immigrant who emerges from the steerage presents such a case. For the alien, whatever ethnic or geographic label he carries, in a primary classification of the creatures of the earth, falls in the human family. The fundamental fact of his humanity established, we need only rehearse the articles of our political faith to know what to do with the immigrant. It is written in our basic law that he is entitled to life, liberty, and the pursuit of happiness. There is nothing left for us to do but to open wide our gates and set him on his way to happiness.

That is what we did for a while, when our simple law was fresh in our minds, and the habit of applying it instinctive. Then there arose a fashion of spelling immigration with a capital initial, which so confused the national eye that we began to see a Problem where formerly we had seen a familiar phenomenon of American life; and as a problem requires skillful handling, we called an army of experts in consultation, and the din of their elaborate discussions has filled our ears ever since.

The effect on the nation has been disastrous. In a matter involving our faith as Americans, we have ceased to consult our fundamental law, and have suffered ourselves to be guided by the conflicting reports of commissions and committees, anthropologists, economists, and statisticians, policy-mongers, calamity-howlers, and self-announced prophets. Matters irrelevant to the interests of liberty have taken the first place in the discussion; lobbyists, not patriots, have had the last word. Our American sensibility has become dulled, so that sometimes the cries of the oppressed have not reached our ears unless carried by formal deputations. In a department of government which brings us into daily touch with the nations of the world, we have failed to live up to our national gospel and have not been aware of our backsliding.

What have the experts and statisticians done so to pervert our minds? They have filled volumes with facts and figures, comparing the immigrants of to-day with the immigrants of other days, classifying them as to race, nationality, and culture, tabulating their occupations, analyzing their savings, probing their motives, prophesying their ultimate destiny. But what is there in all this that bears on the right of free men to choose their place of residence? Granted that Sicilians are not Scotchmen, how does that affect the right of a Sicilian to travel in pursuit of happiness? Strip the alien down to his anatomy, you still find a *man*, a creature made in the image of God; and concerning such a one we have definite instructions from the founders of the Republic. And what purpose was served by the bloody tide of the Civil War if it did not wash away the last lingering doubts as to the brotherhood of men of different races?

There is no impropriety in gathering together a mass of scientific and sociological data concerning the newcomers, as long as we understand that the knowledge so gained is merely the technical answer to a number of technical questions. Where we have gone wrong is in applying the testimony of our experts to the moral side of the question. By all means register the cephalic index of the alien,—the anthropologist will make something of it at his leisure,—but do not let it determine his right to life, liberty, and the pursuit of happiness.

I do not ask that we remove all restrictions and let the flood of immigration sweep in unchecked. I do ask that such restrictions as we impose shall accord with the loftiest interpretation of our duty as Americans. Now our first duty is to live up to the gospel of liberty, through the political practices devised by our forefathers and modified by their successors, as democratic ideas developed. But political practices require a territory wherein to operate—democracy must have standing-room—so it becomes our next duty to guard our frontiers. For that purpose we maintain two forms of defense: the barbaric devices of army and navy, to ward off hostile mass invasions; and the humane devices of the immigration service, to regulate the influx of peaceable individuals.

We have plenty of examples to copy in our military defenses, but when it comes to the civil branch of our national guard, we dare not borrow foreign models. What our neighbors are doing in the matter of regulating immigration may or may not be right for us. Other nations may be guided chiefly by economic considerations, while we are under spiritual bonds to give first consideration to the moral principles involved. For this, our peculiar American problem, we must seek a characteristically American solution.

What terms of entry may we impose on the immigrant without infringing on his inalienable rights, as defined in our national charter? Just such as we would impose on our own citizens if they proposed to move about the country in companies numbering thousands, with their families and portable belongings. And what would these conditions be? They would be such as are required by public safety, public health, public order. Whatever limits to our personal liberty we are ourselves willing to endure for the sake of the public welfare, we have a right to impose on the stranger from abroad; these, and no others.

Has, then, the newest arrival the same rights as the established citizen? According to the Declaration, yes; the same right to live, to move, to try his luck. More than this he does not claim at the gate of entrance; with less than this we are not authorized to put him off. We do not question the right of an individual foreigner to enter our country on any peaceable errand; why, then, question the rights of a shipload of foreigners? Lumping a thousand men together under the title of immigrants does not deprive them of their humanity and the rights inherent in humanity; or can it be demonstrated that the sum of the rights of a million men is less than the rights of one individual?

The Declaration of Independence, like the Ten Commandments, must be taken literally and applied universally. What would have been the civilizing power of the Mosaic Code if the Children of Israel had repudiated it after a few generations? As little virtue is there in the Declaration of Independence if we limit its operation to any geographical sphere or historical period or material situation. How do we belittle the works of our Fathers when we talk as though they wrought for their contemporaries only! It was no great matter to shake off the rule of an absent tyrant, if that is all that the War of the Revolution did. So much had been done many times over, long before the first tree fell under the axe of a New England settler. Emmaus was fought before Yorktown, and Thermopylæ before Emmaus. It is only as we dwell on the words of Jefferson and Franklin that the deeds of Washington shine out among the deeds of heroes. In the chronicles of the Jews, Moses has a far higher place than the Maccabæan brothers. And notice that Moses owes his immortality to the unbroken succession of generations who were willing to rule their lives by the Law that fell from his lips. The glory of the Jews is not that they received the Law, but that they kept the Law. The glory of the American people must be that the vision vouchsafed to their fathers they in their turn hold up undimmed to the eyes of successive generations.

To maintain our own independence is only to hug that vision to our own bosoms. If we sincerely believe in the elevating power of liberty, we should hasten to extend the reign of liberty over all mankind. The disciples of Jesus did not sit down in Jerusalem and congratulate each other on having found the Saviour. They scattered over the world to spread the tidings far and wide. We Americans, disciples of the goddess Liberty, are saved the trouble of carrying our gospel to the nations, because the nations come to us.

Right royally have we welcomed them, and lavishly entertained them at the feast of freedom, whenever our genuine national impulses have shaped our immigration policy. But from time to time the national impulse has been clogged by selfish fears and foolish alarms parading under the guise of civic prudence. Ignoring entirely the *rights* of the case, the immigration debate has raged about questions of expediency, as if convenience and not justice were our first concern. At times the debate has been led by men on whom the responsibilities of American citizenship sat lightly, who treated immigration as a question of the division of spoils.

A little attention to the principles involved would have convinced us long ago that an American citizen who preaches wholesale restriction of immigration is guilty of political heresy. The Declaration of Independence accords to *all* men an equal share in the inherent rights of humanity. When we go contrary to that principle, we are not acting as Americans; for, by definition, an American is one who lives by the principles of the Declaration. And we surely violate the Declaration when we attempt to exclude aliens on account of race, nationality, or economic status. "All men" means yellow men as well as white men, men from the South of Europe as well as men from the North of Europe, men who hold kingdoms in pawn, and men who owe for their dinner. We shall have to recall officially the Declaration of Independence before we can lawfully limit the application of its principles to this or that group of men.

Americans of refined civic conscience have always accepted our national gospel in its literal sense. "What becomes of the rights of the excluded?" demanded the younger Garrison, in a noble scolding administered to the restrictionists in 1896.

If a nation has a right to keep out aliens, tell us how many people constitute a nation, and what geographical area they have a right to claim. In the United States, where a thousand millions can live in peace and plenty under just conditions, who gives to seventy millions the right to monopolize the territory? How few can justly own the earth, and deprive those who are landless of the right to life, liberty, and the pursuit of happiness? And what becomes of the rights of the excluded?

If we took our mission seriously,—as seriously, say, as the Jews take theirs,—we should live with a copy of our law at our side, and oblige every man who opened his mouth to teach us, to square his doctrine with the gospel of liberty; and him should we follow to the end who spoke to us in the name of our duties, rather than in the name of our privileges.

The sins we have been guilty of in our conduct of the immigration debate have had their roots in a misconception of our own position in the land. We have argued the matter as though we owned the land, and were, therefore, at liberty to receive or reject the unbidden guests who came to us by thousands. Let any man who lays claim to any portion of the territory of the United States produce his title deed. Are not most of us squatters here, and squatters of recent date at that? The rights of a squatter are limited to the plot he actually occupies and cultivates. The portion of the United States territory that is covered by squatters' claims is only a fraction, albeit a respectable fraction, of the land we govern. In the name of what moral law do we wield a watchman's club over the vast regions that are still waiting to be staked out? The number of American citizens who can boast of ancestral acres is not sufficient to swing a presidential election. For that matter, those whose claims are founded on ancestral tenure should be the very ones to dread an examination of titles. For it would be shown that these few got their lands by stepping into dead men's shoes, while the majority wrenched their estates from the wilderness by the labor of their own hands. In the face of the sturdy American preference for an aristocracy of brain and brawn, the wisest thing the man with a pedigree can do is to scrape the lichens off his family tree. Think of having it shown that he owes the ancestral farmhouse to the deathbed favoritism of some grouchy uncle! Or, worse still, think of tracing the family title to some canny deal with a band of unsophisticated Indians!

No, it will not do to lay claim to the land on the ground of priority of occupation, as long as there is a red man left on the Indian reservations. If it comes to calling names, usurper is an uglier name than alien. And a squatter is a tenant who doesn't pay any rent, while an immigrant who occupies a tenement in the slums pays his rent regularly or gets out.

We may soothe our pride with the reflection that our title to the land does not depend on the moral validity of individual claims, but on the collective right of the nation to control the land we govern. We came into our land as other nations came into theirs: we took it as a prize of war. Until humanity has devised a less brutal method of political acquisition, we must pass our national claim as entirely sound. We own the land because we were strong enough to take it from England. But the moment we hark back to the War of the Revolution, our sense of possession is profoundly modified. We did not quarrel with the English about the possession of the colonies, but about their treatment of the colonists. It was not a land-grab that was plotted in Independence Hall in 1776, but a pattern of human freedom. We entered upon the war in pursuit of ideals, not in pursuit of homesteads. We had to take the homesteads, too, because, as we have already noted, a political ideal has to have territory wherein to operate. But we must never forget that the shining prize of that war was an immaterial thing,—the triumph of an idea. Not the Treaty of Paris, but the Declaration of Independence, converted the thirteen colonies into a nation.

Having taken half a continent in the name of humanity, shall we hold it in the name of a few millions? Not as jealous lords of a rich domain, but as priests of a noble cult shall we best acquit ourselves of the task our Fathers set us. And it is the duty of a priest to minister to as many souls as he can reach. The most revered of our living teachers has passed this word:—

It is the mission of the United States to spread freedom throughout the world by teaching as many men and women as possible in freedom's largest home how to use freedom rightly through practice in liberty under law.

And our ardor shall not be dampened by the reflection that perhaps the Fathers builded better than they knew. "Do you really think they looked so far ahead?" it is often asked. "Did the founders of the Republic foresee the time when foreign hordes would alight on our shores, demanding a share in this goodly land that was ransomed with the blood of heroes?" Fearful questions, these, to make us pause in the work of redeeming mankind! If our Fathers did not foresee the whole future, shall we therefore be blind to the light of our own day? If they had left us a mere sketch of their idea, could we do less than fill in the outlines? Since they left us not a sketch, but a finished model, the least we can do is to go on copying it on an ever larger scale. Neither shall we falter because the execution of the enlarged copy entails much labor on us and on our children. When Moses told the Egyptian exiles that they should have no god but the One God, he may not have guessed that their children would be brought to the stake for refusing other gods; and yet nineteen centuries of Jewish martyrdom go to show that the followers of Moses did not make his lack of foresight an excuse for abandoning his Law.

Let the children be brought up to know that we are a people with a mission, and that mission, in the words of Dr. Eliot, to teach the uses of freedom to as many men as possible "in freedom's largest home." Let it be taught in the public schools that the most precious piece of real estate in the whole United States is that which supports the pedestal of the Statue of Liberty; that we need not greatly care how the three million square miles remaining is divided among the people of the earth, as long as we retain that little island. Let it further be repeated in the schools that the Liberty at our gates is the handiwork of a Frenchman; that the mountain-weight of copper in her sides and the granite mass beneath her feet were bought with the pennies of the poor; that the verses graven on a tablet within the base are the inspiration of a poetess descended from Portuguese Jews; and all these things shall be interpreted to mean that the love of liberty unites all races and all classes of men into one close brotherhood, and that we Americans, therefore, who have the utmost of liberty that has yet been attained, owe the alien a brother's share.

* * * * *

To this position we are brought by a construction of the Declaration of Independence which makes of it the law of the land, binding on American citizens individually and collectively, and in all circumstances whatever. Out of this position there is one avenue of escape, and only one. We may refuse to read in the Declaration a sincere expression of the faith of 1776, and construe it instead as a bombastic political manifesto, advanced by the leaders of the rebellion as an excuse for a gigantic land-grab.

Let the descendants of the Puritans take their choice of these two interpretations. For my part, I have chosen. I have chosen to read the story of '76 as a chapter in sacred history; to set Thomas Jefferson in a class with Moses, and Washington with Joshua; to regard the American nation as the custodian of a sacred trust, and American citizenship as a holy order, with laws and duties derived from the Declaration.

For very pride in my country I must choose thus, for the alternate view takes the meaning out of American history, reduces the War of Independence to a war of plunder, and the Colonial heroes to a band of pious hypocrites. What, indeed, shall we teach our children to be proud of if we reject the higher interpretation of the deeds of the Fathers? The American Revolution as a campaign of conquest is not unique in history; on the contrary, it has been more than once surpassed, both in respect to the prowess of the conquerors and to the magnificence of the prize. Outside the physical realm, where our inventions and discoveries and the material development of a continent belong, this country has contributed nothing of moment to the world's progress, unless it is that political adaptation of the Golden Rule which is indicated in the Declaration and elaborated in the Constitution. In the arts and sciences we sit, for the most part, at the feet of foreign masters; in jurisprudence we have borrowed from the Romans, and the elements of liberal government we have from our next of kin, the English. The notion of the dignity of man, which is the foundation of the gospel of democracy, is derived from Hebrew sources, as the Psalm-singing founders of New England would be the first to acknowledge. It was not entirely due to accident nor to the exigencies of pioneer life that the meeting-house and the town hall were one in the New England settlements. The influence of the Bible is plainly stamped on the works of the Puritans. What, then, shall we claim as the great American achievement, our peculiar treasure in the midst of so much borrowed glory? A magnificent espousal of humanity—that or nothing can we call our own.

Seeing that they brought nothing into the world that was all their own, our glorious dead are not glorious unless we make them so, by imputing to them the noblest motives that their case will permit, and rating their works at not less than face value. Pride demands it, and, fortunately for our country's honor, justice supports the claims of pride. Neither the cynics nor the enthusiasts shall have the last word in the matter. In the writings of their contemporaries, in the casual sayings of their intimates, in the critical comments of those who came next after them, we find convincing evidence that in the minds of the leaders of '76 the most advanced political thought of the age crystallized into a mighty conviction—the conviction of the inherent nobility of humankind, which makes it treason for any man to enslave his neighbor.

That is the thought that was sent out into the world on July 4, 1776, and because that thought has shaped our history, we call it the basic law of our land, and the Declaration of Independence our final authority. If under that authority the immigrant appears to have rights in our land parallel to our own rights, we shall not lightly deny his claims, lest we forfeit our only title to national glory.

II

JUDGES IN THE GATE

Judges and officers shalt thou make thee in all thy gates . . . and they shall judge the people with just judgment.

DEUT. XVI, 18.

THERE is nothing so potent in a public debate as the picturesque catchwords in which leaders of thought sum up their convictions. Logic makes fewer converts in a year than a taking phrase makes in a week. For catchwords are the popular substitute for logic, and the man in the street is reduced to silence by a good round phrase of the kind that sticks.

Two classes of citizens are especially prone to fall under the tyranny of phrases: those whose horizon, through no fault of their own, is limited by the rim of an empty dinner-pail; and those whose view of the universe is obstructed by the kitchen-middens of too many dinners. There is no clear thinking on an empty stomach, and equally muddled are the thoughts of the over-full. When I hear of a public measure that is largely supported by these two classes of citizens, I know at once that the measure appeals to human prejudices rather than to divine reason.

Thus I became suspicious of the restrictionist movement when I realized that it was in greatest favor among the thoughtless poor and the thoughtless rich. I am well aware that the high-priests of the cult include some of the most conscientious thinkers that ever helped to make history, and their earnestness is attested by a considerable body of doctrine, in support of which they quote statistics and special studies and scientific investigations. But I notice that the rank and file of restrictionists do not know as much as the titles of these documents. They have not followed the argument at all; they have only caught the catchwords of restrictionism. And these catchwords are the sort that appeal to the mean spots in human nature,—the distrust of the stranger, the jealousy of possession, the cowardice of the stomach. Nothing else is expressed by such phrases as "the scum of Europe," "the exploitation of America's wealth," or "taking the bread from the mouth of the American workingman."

Even the least venomous formula of restrictionism, "immigration isn't what it used to be," raises such a familiar echo of foolish human nature that I am bound to challenge its veracity. Does not every generation cry that the weather isn't what it used to be, children are not what they used to be, society is not what it used to be? "The good old times" and "the old immigration" may be twin illusions of limited human vision.

If it is true that immigration is not what it used to be, the fact will appear from a detailed comparison of the "old" and the "new" immigration. But which of the immigrant stocks of the good old times shall be taken as a standard? Woman's wisdom urges me to go right back to the original pattern, just as I would do if I went to the shops to match samples. And the original pattern was brought to this country in the year 1620. Surely comparison with the Mayflower stock is the most searching test of the quality of our immigration that any one could propose.

The predominant virtue of the Pilgrims was idealism. The things of the spirit were more to them than the things of the flesh. May we say the like of our present immigrants? Of very many of them, yes; a thousand times yes. Of the 8,213,000 foreigners landed between the years 1899 and 1909, 990,000 were of that race which for nineteen centuries has sacrificed its flesh in the service of the spirit. It takes a hundred times as much steadfastness and endurance for a Russian Jew of to-day to remain a Jew as it took for an English Protestant in the seventeenth century to defy the established Church.

Those who think that with the Spanish Inquisition Jewish martyrdom came to an end are asked to remember that the Kishinieff affair is only eight years behind us, and that Bielostock has been heard from since Kishinieff, and Mohileff since Bielostock. And more terrible than the recurrent *pogrom*, which hacks and burns and tortures a few hundreds now and then, is the continuous bloodless martyrdom of the six million Jews in Russia through the operation of the anti-Semitic laws of that country. Thirty minutes spent in looking over a summary of these laws recently compiled by an English historian[1] will convince any reader with a spark of imagination that every Russian Jewish immigrant to-day is a fugitive from religious persecution, even as were the English immigrants of 1620.

But while nobody questions the idealism of the Jew in religion, the world has been very slow to credit him with any degree of civic devotion. The world did not stop to think that a man has to have a country before he can prove himself a good citizen. But happily in recent times he has been put to the test of civic opportunity, notably in America; with the result that he was found to possess a fair share of the civic virtues, from the generosity displayed in the town meeting, when citizens vote away their substance to support a public cause, to the brute heroism of the battle-field, where mangled flesh gives proof of valiant spirit.[2] And what the Jews of West European stock proved in the American wars for freedom the Jews of Eastern Europe have proved more recently, by their forwardness in the Russian revolution of 1905.

No group of people of all the heterogeneous mass that constitutes the Russian nation were half so prominent as the Jews in that abortive attempt at freedom. Witness the police records of the revolutionary period, which show that sixty-five out of every hundred political offenders were Jews, in districts where the population was fifteen parts Jewish and eighty-five parts

Gentile. When I visited my native town in the Pale, several years after the revolution, it was hard to find, among the young men and women I talked with, one in a dozen who had not shared in the dangers of 1905. If we really want to know how heartily the Jews played their part in the revolution, we need only ask the Russian Government why the anti-Semitic laws have been so vengefully enforced since a certain crimson year within the present decade. And the whole significance of these things, in the present study, lies in the fact that precisely that spirit which prompts to rebellion in despotic Russia rallies in free America to the support of existing institutions.

If it was a merit in 1620 to flee from religious persecution, and in 1776 to fight against political oppression, then many of the Russian refugees of to-day are a little ahead of the Mayflower troop, because they have in their own lifetime sustained the double ordeal of fight and flight, with all their attendant risks and shocks.

To obtain a nice balance between the relative merits of these two groups of rebels, we remind ourselves that, for sheer adventurousness, migration to America to-day is not to be mentioned on the same page with the magnificent exploit of 1620, and we reflect that the moral glory of the revolution of 1776 is infinitely greater than that of any subsequent revolt; because that, too, was a path-finding adventure, with no compass but faith, no chart but philosophical invention. On the other hand, it is plain that the Russian revolutionists moved against greater odds than the American colonists had to face. The Russians had to plot in secret, assemble in the dark, and strike with bare fists; all this under the very nose of the Czar, with the benighted condition of the Russian masses hanging like a cloud over their enterprise. The colonists were able to lay the train of revolution in the most public manner, they had the local government in their hands, a considerable militia obedient to their own captains, and the advantage of distance from the enemy's resources, with a populace advanced in civic experience promising support to the leaders.

And what a test of heroism was that which the harsh nature of the Russian Government afforded! The American rebels risked their charters and their property; for some of them dungeons waited, and for the leaders dangled a rope, no doubt. But confiscation is not so bitter as Siberian exile, and a halter is less painful than the barbed whip of the Cossacks. The Minutemen at Concord Bridge defied a bully; the rioters in St. Petersburg challenged a tiger. And first of all to be thrust into the cage would be the rebels of Jewish faith, and nobody knew that better than the Jews themselves.

The superior zeal and high degree of self-sacrifice displayed by the Jewish revolutionists would naturally be explained by the fact that, of all the peoples held in chains by the Russian Government, the Jews are the ones who have suffered the cruelest oppression. But there is proof, proof that will go down with the stream of history, that the Jewish participants in the Russian revolution of 1905 were actuated by the highest patriotism, their peculiar grievances being forgotten in the grievances of the nation as a whole. The sinking of the Jewish question in the national question was an important article of the revolutionary propaganda among the Jews; so much so, that when a prominent Jewish leader attempted to demonstrate, on philosophical grounds, that that was a false position to take, he was hotly repudiated, although up to that time he had stood high in the councils of the leaders.[3]

If we find such a high degree of civic responsiveness in what we have been trained to think the most unlikely quarter, shall we not look hopefully in other corners of our world of immigrants? If the Jewish spirit of freedom leaps from the grave of Barkochla to the hovels of the Russian ghetto, half across the world and half across the civilized era, shall we not look for similar prodigies from the more recent graves of Kosciuszko and Garibaldi? If the hook-nosed tailor can turn hero on occasion, why not the grinning organ-grinder, and the surly miner, and the husky lumber-jack? We experienced a shock of surprise, a little while ago, when troops of our Greek immigrants deserted the bootblacking parlors and fruit-stands and tumbled aboard anything that happened to sail for the Mediterranean, in their eagerness—it's hard to bring it out, in connection with a "Dago" bootblack!—in their eagerness to strike a blow for their country in her need.

But that's the worst of calling names: it deceives those who do so. The little bootblacks would not have fooled us as they did if we had not recklessly summed up the Greek character in a contemptuous epithet. It is quite proper for street urchins to invent nicknames for everybody—that is what street urchins are for; but let us not hand down the judgment of the gutter where the judgment of the senate is called for. Between Leonidas at the pass and little Metro under the saloon window, fawning for our nickels, is indeed a dismal gap; and yet Metro, when occasion demanded, reached out his grimy hand and touched the tunic of the Spartan hero.

From these unexpected exploits of the craven Jew and the degenerate Greek, it would seem as if the different elements of the despised "new" immigration only await a spectacular opportunity to prove themselves equal to the "old" in civic valor. But if contemporary history fails to provide a war or revolution for each of our foreign nationalities, we are still not without the means of gauging the idealistic capacity of the aliens. Next after liberty, the Puritans loved education; and to-day, if you examine the registers of the schools and colleges they founded, you will find the names of recent immigrants thickly sprinkled from A to Z, and topping the honor ranks nine times out of ten. All readers of newspapers know the bare facts,—each commencement season, the prize-winners are announced in a string of unpronounceable foreign names; and every school-teacher in the immigrant section of the larger cities has a collection of picturesque anecdotes to contribute: of heroic sacrifices for the sake of a little reading and writing; of young girls stitching away their youth to keep a brother in college; of whole families cheerfully starving together to save one gifted child from the factory.

Go from the public school to the public library, from the library to the social settlement, and you will carry away the same story in a hundred different forms. The good people behind the desks in these public places are fond of repeating that they can hardly keep up with the intellectual demands of their immigrant neighbors. In the experience of the librarians it is the veriest commonplace that the classics have the greatest circulation in the immigrant quarters of the city; and the most touching proof of reverence for learning often comes from the illiterate among the aliens. On the East Side of New York, "Teacher" is a being adored. Said a bedraggled Jewish mother to her little boy who had affronted his teacher, "Don't you know that teachers is holy?" Perhaps these are the things the teachers have in mind when they speak with a tremor of the immense reward of work in the public schools.

That way of speaking is the fashion among workers of all sorts in the educational institutions where foreigners attend in numbers. Get a group of settlement people swapping anecdotes about their immigrant neighbors, and there is apt to develop an epidemic of moist eyes. Out of the fullness of their knowledge these social missionaries pay the tribute of respect and affection to the strangers among whom they toil. For they know them as we know our brothers and sisters, from living and working and rejoicing and sorrowing together.

The testimony of everyday experience is borne out by the sudden revelations of catastrophic circumstances, as reported by a librarian from Dayton, Ohio. In Dayton they had branch libraries located in different parts of the city, not in separate library buildings, but in convenient shops or dwelling-houses, where they were left in the care of some responsible person in the neighborhood. After the recent flood,[4] when the panic was over and the people began to dig for their belongings underneath the accumulated slime and wreckage, the librarian tried to collect at the central library whatever was recovered of the scattered collection. Crumpled, mutilated, slimy with the filth of the disemboweled city, the books came back—all but one collection, which had been housed in the midst of the Hungarian quarter. These came back neatly packed, scraped clean of mud, their leaves smoothed, dried,—as presentable as loving care could make them.

If that was not a manifestation of pure idealism, then is human conduct void of symbolism, and our public squares are cumbered in vain with monuments erected in commemoration of human deeds. But we read men's souls in their actions, and we know that they who flock to the schools are the spiritual kindred of those who founded them; they who cherish a book are passing along the torch kindled by him who wrote it. They pay the highest tribute to an inventor who show the most eagerness to adopt his invention. The great New England invention of compulsory education is more eagerly appropriated by the majority of our immigrants than by native Americans of the corresponding level. That is what the school-teachers say, and I suppose they know. They also say,—they and all public educators in chorus,—that while one foreign nationality excels in the love of letters, another excels in the love of music, and a third in the love of science; and all of them together constitute an army whose feet keep time with the noble rhythms of culture.

Let a New Yorker on Friday night watch the crowd pushing out of a concert hall after one of Ysaye's recitals, and on Saturday afternoon let him take the subway uptown, and get out where the crowd gets out, and buy a ticket for the baseball game. If he can keep cool enough for a little study, let him compare the distorted faces in the bleachers with the shining faces of the crowd of the night before; and let him say which crowd responded to the nobler inspiration, and then let him declare in which group the foreigners outnumbered the Americans.

The American devotion to sport is no reproach to the descendants of the Puritans, since it can be demonstrated from various angles that the baseball diamond may supplement the schoolroom and the pulpit in the training of American citizens. Indeed, it is not difficult to accept that interpretation of the national sport which reduces a good game of baseball to an epitome of all that is best in the lives of the best Americans. At the same time we need to remember that the love of art is more generally accepted as a mark of grace than the love of sport. Thus, when we speak of the glory of old Athens we have in mind not the Olympian games, noble as they were, but the poets and sculptors and philosophers who uttered her thoughts. The original of the Discobolus must have been a winner,—I can imagine Athenian mothers lifting up their beautiful bare babies to see the hero over the heads of the throng,—but who can tell me his name to-day? Meanwhile the name of Myron has been guarded as a talisman of civilization.

We shall not look in the sporting columns, then, for the names of contemporary Americans who are likely to secure us a place of honor on the scrolls of history. We look under the current book reviews, in theatre programmes, in the announcements of art galleries. As a by-product of such a search we announce the discovery that the prizefighters seem to be near cousins of certain Americans of turbulent notoriety in politics, themselves derived from one of the approved immigrant stocks of the "old" dispensation; while the singer and painter and writer folk very often hail from those parts of Europe at present labeled "undesirable" as a source of immigration. Nay, is it not a good joke on the restrictionists that an American singer who aspires to be a prima donna must trick herself out with a name borrowed from the steerage lists of recent arrivals at Ellis Island?

If it is the scum of Europe that we are getting in our present immigration, it seems to be a scum rich in pearls. Pearl-fishing, of course, is accompanied by labor and danger and expense, but it is reckoned a paying industry, or practical men would not invest their capital in it. The brunt of the business falls on the divers, however. Have we divers willing to go down into our human sea and risk an encounter with sharks and grope in the ooze at the bottom? We have our school teachers and librarians and social missionaries, whose zest for their work should shame us out of counting the cost of our human fishery. As to the accumulations of empty shells, we are told that in the pearl fisheries of South America about one oyster in a thousand yields a pearl; and yet the industry goes on.

The lesson of the oyster bank goes further still. We know that the nine hundred and ninety-nine empty shells have a lining, at least, of mother-of-pearl. We are thus encouraged to look for the generic opalescence of humanity in the undistinguished mass of our immigrants. What do the aliens show of the specific traits of manhood that go to the making of good citizens? Immersed in the tide of American life, do their spiritual secretions give off that fine lustre of manhood that distinguished the noble Pilgrims of the first immigration? The genius of the few is obvious; the group virtue of the mass on exalted occasions, such as popular uprisings, has been sufficiently demonstrated. What we want to know now is whether the ordinary immigrant under ordinary circumstances comes anywhere near the type we have taken as a model.

There can be no effective comparison between the makers of history of a most romantic epoch and the venders of bananas on our own thrice-commonplace streets. But the Pilgrims were not always engaged in signing momentous compacts or in effecting a historic landing. In a secondary capacity they were immigrants—strangers come to establish themselves in a strange land—and as such they may profitably be used as a model by which to measure other immigrants.

The historic merit of their enterprise aside, the virtue of the Pilgrim Fathers was that they came not to despoil, but to build; that they resolutely turned their backs on conditions of life that galled them, and set out to make their own conditions in a strange and untried world, at great hazard to life and limb and fortune; that they asked no favors of God, but paid in advance for His miracles, by hewing and digging and ploughing and fighting against odds; that they respected humankind, believed in themselves, and pushed the business of the moment as if the universe hung on the result.

The average immigrant of to-day, like the immigrant of 1620, comes to build—to build a civilized home under a civilized government, which diminishes the amount of barbarity in the world. He, too, like that earlier newcomer, has rebelled against the conditions of his life, and adventured halfway across the world in search of more acceptable conditions, facing exile and uncertainty and the terrors of the untried. He also pays as he goes along, and in very much the same coin as did the Pilgrims; awaiting God's miracle of human happiness in the grisly darkness of the mine, in the fierce glare of the prairie ranch, in the shrivelling heat of coke-ovens, beside roaring cotton-gins, beside blinding silk-looms, in stifling tailor-shops, in nerve-racking engine-rooms,—in all those places where the assurance and pride of the State come to rest upon the courage and patience of the individual citizen.

There is enough of peril left in the adventure of emigration to mark him who undertakes it as a man of some daring and resource. Has civilization smoothed the sea, or have not steamships been known to founder as well as sailing vessels? Does not the modern immigrant also venture among strangers, who know not his ways nor speak his tongue nor worship his God? If his landing is not threatened by savages in ambush, he has to run the gauntlet of exacting laws that serve not his immediate interests. The early New England farmer used to carry his rifle with him in the fields, to be ready for prowling Indians, and the gutter-merchant of New York to-day is obliged to carry about the whole armory of his wits, to avert the tomahawk of competition. No less cruel than Indian chiefs to their white captives is the greedy industrial boss to the laborers whom poverty puts at his mercy; and how could you better match the wolves and foxes that prowled about the forest clearings of our ancestors than by the pack of sharpers and misinformers who infest the immigrant quarters of our cities?

Measured by the exertions necessary to overcome them, the difficulties that beset the modern immigrant are no less formidable than those which the Pilgrims had to face. There has never been a time when it was more difficult to get something for nothing than it is to-day, but the unromantic setting of modern enterprises leads us to underestimate the moral qualities that make success possible to-day. Undoubtedly the pioneer with an axe over his shoulder is a more picturesque figure than the clerk with a pencil behind his ear, but we who have stood up against the shocks of modern life should know better than to confuse the picturesque with the heroic. Do we not know that it takes a *man* to beat circumstances, to-day as in the days of the pioneers? And manliness is always the same mixture of courage, self-reliance, perseverance, and faith.

Inventions have multiplied since the days of the Pilgrims, but which of our mechanical devices takes the place of the old-fashioned quality of determination where obstacles are to be overcome? The New England wilderness retreated not before the axe, but before the diligence of the men who wielded the axe; and diligence it is which to-day transmutes the city's refuse into a loaf for the ragpicker's children. Resourcefulness—the ability to adjust the means to the end—enters equally in the subtle enterprises of the business man and in the hardy exploits of the settler; and it takes as much patience to wait for returns on a petty investment of capital as it does to watch the sprouting of an acre of corn.

Hardiness and muscle and physical courage were the seventeenth-century manifestations of the same moral qualities which to-day are expressed as intensity and nerve and commercial daring. Our country being in part cultivated, in part savage, we need citizens with the endowment of the twentieth century, and citizens with the pioneer endowment. The "new" immigration, however interpreted, consists in the main of these two types.

Whether we get these elements in the proportion best suited to our needs is another question, to be answered in its place. At this point it is only necessary to admit that the immigrant possesses an abundance of the homely virtues of the useful citizen in times of peace.

We arrived at this conclusion by a theoretical analysis of the qualities that carry a man through life to-day; and that was fair reasoning, since the great majority of aliens are known to make good, if not in the first generation, then in the second or the third. Any sociologist, any settlement worker, any census clerk will tell you that the history of the average immigrant family of the "new" period is represented by an ascending curve. The descending curves are furnished by degenerate families of what was once prime American stock. I want no better proof of these facts than I find in the respective vocabularies of the missionary in the slums of New York and the missionary in the New England hills. At the settlement on Eldridge Street they talk about hastening the process of Americanization of the immigrant; the country minister in the Berkshires talks about the rehabilitation of the Yankee farmer. That is, the one assists at an upward process, the other seeks to reverse a downward process.

Right here, in these opposite tendencies of the poor of the foreign quarters and the poor of the Yankee fastnesses, I read the most convincing proof that what we get in the steerage is not the refuse, but the sinew and bone of all the nations. If rural New England to-day shows signs of degeneracy, it is because much of her sinew and bone departed from her long ago. Some of the best blood of New England answered to the call of "Westward ho!" when the empty lands beyond the Alleghanies gaped for population, while on the spent farms of the Puritan settlements too many sons awaited the division of the father's property. Of those who were left behind, many, of course, were detained by habit and sentiment, love of the old home being stronger in them than the lure of adventure. Of the aristocracy of New England that portion stayed at home which was fortified by wealth, and so did not feel the economic pressure of increased population; of the proletariat remained, on the whole, the less robust, the less venturesome, the men and women of conservative imagination.

It was bound to be so, because, wherever the population is set in motion by internal pressure, the emigrant train is composed of the stoutest, the most resourceful of those who are not held back by the roots of wealth or sentiment. Voluntary emigration always calls for the highest combination of the physical and moral virtues. The law of analogy, therefore, might suffice to teach us that with every shipload of immigrants we get a fresh infusion of pioneer blood. But theory is a tight-rope on which every monkey of a logician can balance himself. We practical Americans of the twentieth century like to feel the broad platform of tested facts beneath our feet.

The fact about the modern immigrant is that he is everywhere continuing the work begun by our pioneer ancestors. So much we may learn from a bare recital of the occupations of aliens. They supply most of the animal strength and primitive patience that are at the bottom of our civilization. In California they gather the harvest, in Arizona they dig irrigation ditches, in Oregon they fell forests, in West Virginia they tunnel coal, in Massachusetts they plant the tedious crops suitable to an exhausted soil. In the cities they build subways and skyscrapers and railroad terminals that are the wonder of the world. Wherever rough work and low wages go together, we have a job for the immigrant.

ROUGH WORK AND LOW WAGES FOR THE IMMIGRANT

The prouder we grow, the more we lean on the immigrant. The Wall Street magnate would be about as effective as a puppet were it not for the army of foreigners who execute his schemes. The magic of stocks and bonds lies in railroad ties and in quarried stone and in axle grease applied at the right time. A Harriman might sit till doomsday gibbering at the telephone and the stock exchange would take no notice of him if a band of nameless "Dagos" a thousand miles away failed to repair a telegraph pole. New York City is building an aqueduct that will surpass the works of the Romans, and the average New Yorker will know nothing about it until he reads in the newspapers the mayor's speech at the inauguration of the new water supply.

Our brains, our wealth, our ambitions flow in channels dug by the hands of immigrants. Alien hands erect our offices, rivet our bridges, and pile up the proud masonry of our monuments. Ignoring in this connection the fact that the engineer as well as the laborer is often of alien race, we owe to mere muscle a measure of recognition proportionate to our need of muscle in our boasted material progress. An imaginative schoolboy left to himself must presently catch the resemblance between the pick-and-shovel men toiling at our aqueducts and the heroes of the axe and rifle extolled in his textbooks as the "sturdy pioneers." Considered without prejudice, the chief difference between these two types is the difference between jean overalls and fringed buckskins. Contemporaneousness takes the romance out of everything; otherwise we might be rubbing elbows with heroes. Whatever merit there was in hewing and digging and hauling in the days of the first settlers still inheres in the same operations to-day. Yes, and a little extra; for a stick of dynamite is more dangerous to handle than a crowbar, and the steam engine makes more widows in a year than ever the Indian did with bloody tomahawk and stealthy arrow.

There is no contention here that every fellow who successfully passes the entrance ordeals at Ellis Island is necessarily a hero. That there are weaklings in the train of the sturdy throng of foreigners nobody knows better than I. I have witnessed the pitiful struggles of the unfit, and have seen the failures drop all around me. But no bold army ever marched to the field of action without a fringe of camp-followers on its flanks. The moral vortex created by the enterprises of the resolute sucks in a certain number of the weak-hearted; and this is especially true in mass movements, where the enthusiasm of the crowd ekes out the courage of the individual. If it is not too impious to suggest it, may there not have been among the passengers of the Mayflower two or three or half a dozen who came over because their cousins did, not because they had any zest for the adventure?

When we remember that the Pilgrim Fathers came with their families, we may be very sure that that was the case, because the different members of a family are seldom of the same moral fibre. No doubt the austere ambitions of the voyagers of the Mayflower made them stern recruiting masters, but our knowledge of men in the mass forbids the assumption that they were all heroes of the first rank who stepped ashore on Plymouth Rock.

I have little sympathy with declaimers about the Pilgrim Fathers, who look upon them all as men of grand conceptions and superhuman foresight. An entire ship's company of Columbuses is what the world never saw.

It takes a wizard critic like Lowell to chip away the crust of historic sentiment and show us our forefathers in the flesh. Lowell would agree with me that the Pilgrims were a picked troop in the sense that there was an immense preponderance of virtue among them. And that is exactly what we must say of our modern immigrants, if we judge them by the sum total of their effect on our country.

Not a little of the glory of the Pilgrim Fathers rests on their own testimony. Our opinion of them is greatly enhanced by the expression we find, in the public and private documents they have left us, of their ideals, their aims, their expectations in the New World. Let us judge our immigrants also out of their own mouths, as future generations will be sure to judge them. And in seeking this testimony let us remember that humanity in general does not produce one oracle in a decade. Very few men know their own hearts, or can give an account of the impulses that drive them in a particular direction. We put our ears to the lips of the eloquent when we want to know what the world is thinking. And what do we get when we sift down the sayings of the spokesmen among the foreign folk? An anthem in praise of American ideals, a passionate glorification of the principles of democracy.

Let it be understood that the men and women of exceptional intellect, who have surveyed the situation from philosophical heights, are not trumpeting forth their own high dreams alone. If they have won the ear of the American nation and shamed the indifferent and silenced the cynical, it is because they voiced the feeling of the inarticulate mob that welters in the foreign quarters of our cities. I am never so clear as to the basis of my faith in America as when I have been talking with the ungroomed mothers of the East Side. A widow down on Division Street was complaining bitterly of the hardships of her lot, alone in an alien world with four children to bring up. In the midst of her complaints the children came in from school. "Well," said the hard-pressed widow, "bread isn't easy to get in America, but the children can go to school, and that's more than bread. Rich man, poor man, it's all the same: the children can go to school."

The poor widow had never heard of a document called the Declaration of Independence, but evidently she had discovered in American practice something corresponding to one of the great American principles,—the principle of equality of opportunity,—and she valued it more than the necessaries of animal life. Even so was it valued by the Fathers of the Republic, when they deliberately incurred the dangers of a war with mighty England in defense of that and similar principles.

THE UNGROOMED MOTHER OF THE EAST SIDE

The widow's sentiment was finely echoed by another Russian immigrant, a man who drives an ice-wagon for a living. His case is the more impressive from the fact that he left a position of comparative opulence in the old country, under the protection of a wealthy uncle who employed him as steward of his estates. He had had servants to wait on him and money enough to buy some of the privileges of citizenship which the Russian Government doles out to the favored few. "But what good was it to me?" he asked. "My property was not my own if the police wanted to take it away. I could spend thousands to push my boy through the Gymnasium, and he might get a little education as a favor, and still nothing out of it, if he isn't allowed to be anything. Here I work like a slave, and my wife she works like a slave, too,—in the old country she had servants in the house,—but what do I care, as long as I know what I earn I got it for my own? I got to furnish my house one chair at a time, in America, but nobody can take it away from me, the little that I got. And it costs me nothing to educate my family. Maybe they can, maybe they can't go to college, but all can go through grammar school, and high school, too, the smart ones. And all go together! Rich and poor, all are equal, and I don't get it as a favor."

Better a hard bed in the shelter of justice than a stuffed couch under the black canopy of despotism. Better a crust of the bread of the intellect freely given him as his right than the whole loaf grudgingly handed him as a favor. What nobler insistence on the rights of manhood do we find in the writings of the Puritans?

Volumes might be filled with the broken sayings of the humblest among the immigrants which, translated into the sounding terms of the universal, would give us the precious documents of American history over again. Never was the bread of freedom more keenly relished than it is to-day, by the very people of whom it is said that they covet only the golden platter on which it is served up. We may not say that immigration to our country has ceased to be a quest of the ideal as long as the immigrants lay so much stress on the spiritual accompaniment of economic elevation in America. Nobly built upon the dreams of the Fathers, the house of our Republic is nobly tenanted by those who cherish similar dreams.

But dreams cannot be brought before a court of inquiry. A diligent immigration commission with an appropriation to spend has little time to listen to Joseph. A digest of its report is expected to yield statistics rather than rhapsodies. The taxpayers want their money's worth of hard facts.

But when the facts are raked together and boiled down to a summary that the business man may scan on his way to the office, behold! we are no wiser than before. For a host of interpreters jump into the seats vacated by the extinct commission and harangue us in learned terms on the merits and demerits of the immigrant, *as they conceive them*, after studying the voluminous report. That is, the question is still what it was before: a matter of personal opinion! The man with the vote realizes that *he* has to make up *his* mind what instructions to send to his representative in Congress on the subject of immigration. And where shall he, a plain, practical man, unaccustomed to interpret dreams or analyze statistics, find an index of the alien's worth that he can read through the spectacles of common sense?

There is a phrase in the American vocabulary of approval that sums up our national ideal of manhood. That phrase is "a self-made man." To such we pay the tribute of our highest admiration, justly regarding our self-made men as the noblest product of our democratic institutions. Now let any one compile a biographical dictionary of our self-made men, from the romantic age of our history down to the prosaic year 1914, and see how the smell of the steerage pervades the volume! *There* is a sign that the practical man finds it easy to interpret. Like fruits grow from like seeds. Those who can produce under American conditions the indigenous type of manhood must be working with the same elements as the native American who starts out a yokel and ends up a senator.

Focused under the microscope of theoretical analysis, or

viewed through the spectacles of common sense, the average immigrant of to-day still shows the markings of virtue that have distinguished the best Americans from the time of the landing at Plymouth to the opening of the Panama Canal. But popular judgment is seldom based on a study of the norm, especially in this age of the newspaper. The newspaper is devoted to the portrayal of the abnormal—the shining example and the horrible example; and most men think they have done justice when they have balanced the one against the other, leaving out of account entirely the great mass that lies between the two extremes. And even of the two extremes, it is the horrible example that is more frequently brought to the attention of the public. Half a dozen Italians draw knives in a brawl on a given evening, and the morning newspapers are full of the story. On the same evening hundreds of Italians were studying civics in the night schools, inquiring for classics at the public library, rehearsing for a historical pageant at the settlement—and not a word about them in the newspapers. One Jewish gangster makes more "copy" than a hundred Jewish boys and girls who win honors in college. So also it is the business of the police to record the fact that a Greek was arrested for peddling without a license, while it is nobody's business to report that a dozen other Greeks chipped in their spare change to pay his fine. The reader of newspapers is convinced that the foreigners as a whole are a violent, vicious, lawless crowd, and the fewer we have of them the better.

Could the annual reports of libraries and settlements be circulated as widely as the newspapers, the American public would not be guilty of such errors of judgment. But who reads annual reports? The very name of them is forbidding! It becomes necessary, therefore, to explain the newspaper types that jump to the fore in every discussion of the immigrant.

First of all we must get a good grip on our sense of proportion. To speak of the immigrants as undesirable because a few of them throw bombs or live by gambling is about as fair as it would be for the world to call us Americans a nation of dissolute millionaires and industrial pirates because a Harry Thaw drank himself into an insane asylum and a Rockefeller swept a host of competitors to ruin.

But the bomb-thrower and the gambler are extremely undesirable. Look at the Black Hand outrages, look at the Rosenthal case!

Aye, I have looked, and I see plainly that these horrible examples are due to the same causes as any shining example that could be named. Each is the product of the qualities the immigrant brought with him and the opportunities he found here to exercise them. The law-abiding, ambitious immigrant who came here a beggar and worked himself into the ranks of the princes found his opportunity in our laws and customs, which enable the common man to make the most of himself. The blackmailer's opportunity was provided by the operation of corrupt politics, which removes police commissioners and impeaches governors for trying to enforce the law. The Rosenthal case brought forth Lieutenant Becker, and an investigation of the spread of the Black Hand terror discovers political bosses behind the scenes.[5] We have laws providing for the deportation of alien criminals. Why are they not always enforced? When we have found the broom that will sweep the political vermin from our legislatures, we shan't need to look around for a shovel to keep back the scum of Europe. The two will go together.

In the whole catalogue of sins with which the modern immigrant is charged, it is not easy to find one in which we Americans are not partners,—we who can make and unmake our world by means of the ballot. The immigrant is blamed for the unsanitary conditions of the slums, when sanitary experts cry shame on our methods of municipal house-cleaning. You might dump the whole of the East Side into the German capital and there would be no slums there, because the municipal authorities of Berlin know how to enforce building regulations, how to plant trees, and how to clean the streets. The very existence of the slum is laid at the door of the immigrant, but the truth is that the slums were here before the immigrants. Most of the foreigners hate the slums, and all but the few who have no backbone get out of them as fast as they rise in the economic scale. To "move uptown" is the dearest ambition of the average immigrant family.

If the slums were due to the influx of foreigners, why should London have slums, and more hideous slums than New York? No, the slum is not a by-product of the steerage. It is a sore on the social body in many civilized countries, due to internal disorders of the economic system. A generous dose of social reformation would do more to effect a cure than repeated doses of restriction of immigration.

A whole group of phenomena due to social and economic causes have been falsely traced, in this country, to the quantity and quality of immigration. Among these are the labor troubles, such as non-employment, strikes, riots, etc. England has no such immigration as the United States, and yet Englishmen suffer from non-employment, from riots and bitter strikes. Whom does the English workingman blame for his misery? Let the American workingman quarrel with the same enemy. If wage-cutting is a sin more justly laid at the door of the immigrant, a minimum wage law might put a stop to that.

The immigrant undoubtedly contributes to the congestion of population in the cities, but not as a chief cause. Congestion is characteristic of city life the world over, and the remedy will be found in improved conditions of country life. Moreover, the immigrant has shown himself responsive to direction away from the city when a systematic attempt is made to help him find his place in the country. There is the experience of the Industrial Removal Office of the Baron de Hirsch Foundation as a hint of what the Government might accomplish if it took a hand in the intelligent distribution of immigration. The records of this organization, dealing with a group of immigrants supposed to be especially addicted to city life, kill two immigrant myths at one stroke. They prove that it is possible to direct the stream of immigration in desired channels and that the Jew is not altogether averse to contact with the soil; both facts contrary to popular notions.

A good deal of anti-immigration feeling has been based on the vile conditions observed in labor camps, by another turn of that logic which puts the blame on the victims. A labor camp at its worst is not an argument against immigration, but an indictment of the brutality of the contractor who cares only to force a maximum of work out of the workmen, and cares nothing for their lives; an indictment also of the Government that allows such shameful exploitation of the laborers to go on. That a labor camp does not have to be a plague spot has been gloriously demonstrated by Goethals at Panama. What Goethals did was to emphasize the *man* in workingman, with the result that Panama during the vast operations of digging the Canal was a healthier, happier, more inspiring place to live in than many of our proudest cities; the workmen came away from the job better men and better citizens; and the work was better done and with more dispatch and at less expense than any such work was ever done by the old-fashioned method, where the workers are treated not as men but as tools.

There may not be another Goethals in the country, but what a great man devises little men may copy. The labor camp must never again be mentioned as a reproach to the immigrant who suffers degradation in it, or the world will think that we do not know the meaning of the medals which we ourselves have hung on Goethals's breast.

Immigrants are accused of civic indifference if they do not become naturalized, but when we look into the conditions affecting naturalization we wonder at the numbers who do become citizens. Facilities for civic education of the adult are very scant, and dependent mostly on the fluctuating enthusiasm of private philanthropies. The administration of the naturalization laws differs from State to State and is accompanied by serious material hindrances; while the community is so indifferent to the civic progress of its alien members that it is possible for a foreigner to live in this country for *sixteen years*, coming in contact with all classes of Americans, without getting the bare information that he may become a citizen of the United States if he wants to. Such a case, as reported by a charity worker of New Britain, Connecticut, makes a sensitive American choke with mortification. If we were ourselves as patriotic as we expect the immigrant to be, we would employ Salvation Army methods to draw the foreigner into the civic fold. Instead of that, we leave his citizenship to chance—or to the most corrupt political agencies.

I would rather not review the blackest of all charges against the immigrant, that he has a baleful effect on municipal politics: I am so ashamed of the implications. But sensible citizens will talk and talk about the immigrant selling his vote, and not know whom they are accusing. Votes cannot be sold unless there is a market for them. Who creates the market for votes? The ward politician, behind whom stands the party boss, alert, and powerful; and behind him—the indifferent electorate who allow him to flourish.

Among immigrants of the "new" order, the wholesale prostitution of the ballot is confined to those groups which are largely subjected to the industrial slavery of mining and manufacturing communities and construction camps. These helpless creatures, in their very act of sinning, bear twofold witness against us who accuse them. The foreman who disposes of their solid vote acquires his power under an economic system which delivers them up, body and soul, to the man who pays them wages, and turns it to account under a political system which makes the legislature subservient to the stock exchange. But let it be definitely noted that to admit that groups of immigrants under economic control fall an easy prey to political corruptionists is very far from proving any inherent viciousness in the immigrants themselves.

Neither does the immigrant's civic reputation depend entirely on negative evidence. New York City has the largest foreign population in the United States, and precisely in that city the politicians have learned that they cannot count on the foreign vote, because it is not for sale. A student of New York politics speaks of the "uncontrollable and unapproachable vote of the Ghetto." Repeated analyses of the election returns of the Eighth District, which has the largest foreign population of all, show that "politically it is one of the most uncertain sections" in the city. Many generations of campaign managers have discovered to their sorrow that the usual party blandishments are wasted on the East Side masses. Hester Street follows leaders and causes rather than party emblems. Nowhere is the art of splitting a ticket better understood. The only time you can predict the East Side vote is when there is a sharp alignment of the better citizens against the boss-ridden. Then you will find the naturalized citizens in the same camp with men like Jacob Riis and women like Lillian Wald. And the experience of New York is duplicated in Chicago and in Philadelphia and in every center of immigration. Ask the reformers.

How often we demand more civic virtue of the stranger than we ourselves possess! A little more time spent in weeding our own garden will relieve us of the necessity of counting the tin cans in the immigrant's back yard.

As to tin cans, the immigrants are not the only ones who scatter them broadcast. How can we talk about the foreigners defacing public property, when our own bill-boards disfigure every open space that God tries to make beautiful for us? It is true that the East Side crowds litter the parks with papers and fruit-skins and peanut shells, but they would not be able to do so if the park regulations were persistently enforced. And in the mean time the East Side children, in their pageants and dance festivals, make the most beautiful use of the parks that a poet could desire.

There exists a society in the United States the object of which is to protect the natural beauties and historical landmarks of our country. Who are the marauders who have called such a society into being? Who is it that threatens to demolish the Palisades and drain off Niagara? Who are the vulgar folk who scrawl their initials on trees and monuments, who chip off bits from historic tombstones, who profane the holy echoes of the mountains by calling foolish phrases through a megaphone? The officers of the Scenic and Historic Preservation Society are not watching Ellis Island. On the contrary, it was the son of an immigrant whose expert testimony, given before a legislative committee at Albany, helped the Society to save the Falls of the Genesee from devastation by a power company. This same immigrant's son, on another occasion, spent two mortal hours tearing off visiting-cards from a poet's grave—cards bearing the names of American vacationists.

Some of the things we say against the immigrants sound very strange from American lips. We speak of the corruption of our children's manners through contact with immigrant children in the public schools, when all the world is scolding us for our children's rude deportment. Finer manners are grown on a tiny farm in Italy than in the roaring subways of New York; and contrast our lunch-counter manners with the table-manners of the Polish ghetto, where bread must not be touched with unwashed hands, where a pause for prayer begins and ends each meal, and on festival occasions parents and children join in folk-songs between courses!

If there is a corruption of manners, it may be that it works in the opposite direction from what we suppose. At any rate, we ourselves admit that the children of foreigners, before they are Americanized, have a greater respect than our children for the Fifth Commandment.

We say that immigrants nowadays come only to exploit our country, because some of them go back after a few years, taking their savings with them. The real exploiters of our country's wealth are not the foreign laborers, but the capitalists who pay them wages. The laborer who returns home with his savings leaves us an equivalent in the products of labor; a day's service rendered for every day's wages. The capitalists take away our forests and water-courses and mineral treasures and give us watered stock in return.

Of the class of aliens who do not come to make their homes here, but only to earn a few hundred dollars to invest in a farm or a cottage in their native village, a greater number than we imagine are brought over by industrial agents in violation of the contract labor law. Put an end to the stimulation of immigration, and we shall see very few of the class who do not come to stay. And even as it is, not all of those who return to Europe do so in order to spend their American fortune. Some go back to recover from ruin encountered at the hands of American land swindlers. Some go back to be buried beside their fathers, having lost their health in unsanitary American factories. And some are helped aboard on crutches, having lost a limb in a mine explosion that could have been prevented. When we watch the procession of cripples hobbling back to their native villages, it looks more as if America is exploiting Europe.

O that the American people would learn where their enemies lurk! Not the immigrant is ruining our country, but the venal politicians who try to make the immigrant the scapegoat for all the sins of untrammeled capitalism—these and their masters. Find me the agent who obstructs the movement for the abolition of child labor, and I will show you who it is that condemns able-bodied men to eat their hearts out in idleness; who brutalizes our mothers and tortures tender babies; who fills the morgues with the emaciated bodies of young girls, and the infirmaries with little white cots; who fastens the shame of illiteracy on our enlightened land, and causes American boys to grow up too ignorant to mark a ballot; who sucks the blood of the nation, fattens on its brains, and throws its heart to the wolves of the money market.

The stench of the slums is nothing to the stench of the child-labor iniquity. If the foreigners are taking the bread out of the mouth of the American workingman, it is by the maimed fingers of their fainting little ones.

And if we want to know whether the immigrant parents are the promoters or the victims of the child labor system, we turn to the cotton mills, where forty thousand native American children between seven and sixteen years of age toil between ten and twelve hours a day, while the fathers rot in the degradation of idleness.

From all this does it follow that we should let down the bars and dispense with the guard at Ellis Island? Only in so far as the policy of restriction is based on the theory that the present immigration is derived from the scum of humanity. But the immigrants may be desirable and immigration undesirable. We sometimes have to deny ourselves to the most congenial friends who knock at our door. At this point, however, we are not trying to answer the question whether immigration is good for us. We are concerned only with the reputation of the immigrant—and incidentally with the reputation of those who have sought to degrade him in our eyes. If statecraft bids us lock the gate, and our national code of ethics ratifies the order, lock it we must, but we need not call names through the keyhole.

Mount guard in the name of the Republic if the health of the Republic requires it, but let no such order be issued until her statesmen and philosophers and patriots have consulted together. Above all, let the voice of prejudice be stilled, let not self-interest chew the cud of envy in full sight of the nation, and let no syllable of willful defamation mar the oracles of state. For those who are excluded when our bars are down are exiles from Egypt, whose feet stumble in the desert of political and social slavery, whose hearts hunger for the bread of freedom. The ghost of the Mayflower pilots every immigrant ship, and Ellis Island is another name for Plymouth Rock.

III

THE FIERY FURNACE

Nebuchadnezzar spake and said unto them, . . . Now if ye be ready that at what time ye hear the sound of the cornet . . . ye fall down and worship the image that I have made; well: but if ye worship not, ye shall be cast the same hour into the midst of a burning fiery furnace; and who is that God that shall deliver you out of my hands?

Shadrach, Meshach, and Abed-nego, answered and said to the king, O, Nebuchadnezzar, we are not careful to answer thee in this matter. If it be so, our God whom we serve is able to deliver us from the burning fiery furnace, and he will deliver us out of thine hand, O king. But if not, be it known unto thee, O king, that we will not serve thy gods, nor worship the golden image which thou hast set up.

DAN. III, 14-18.

IN the discussion of the third question,—whether immigration is good for us,—more honest Americans have gone astray than in the other two divisions. Let it be said at the outset that those who have erred have been about equally distributed between the ayes and the nays. For the answer to this question is neither aye nor nay, but something that cannot be put into a single syllable. If we steer our way cautiously between the opposing ranks, the light of the true answer will presently shine on us.

The arguments they severally advance in defense of their

respective positions reveal an appalling number of citizens on each side of the house who have entirely disregarded the principles involved. Those who, like the labor-union lobbyists, point to the empty dinner-pails of American workingmen as a reason for keeping out foreign labor, are no more at fault than the lobbyists of the opposite side, who offer in support of the open-door policy statistics showing the need of rough laborers in various branches of our current material development. All of them are wrong in that they would treat our foreign brothers as pawns on the chessboard of our selfish needs. Show me a million American workingmen out of work, and I fail to see a justification for the exclusion of a million men from other lands who are also looking for a job. Does the mother of an impoverished family strangle half her brood in order that the other half may have enough to eat? No; she divides the last crust equally among her starvelings, and the laws of nature do the rest.

This analogy, of course, is a vessel without a bottom unless the gospel of the brotherhood of man is accepted as a premise of our debate. The only logic it will hold is the logic of a practical incarnation of the theories we loudly applaud on occasions of patriotic excitement. That ought to be acceptable both to the poor men who like to parade the streets with the Stars and Stripes at the head of the column and the *Marseillaise* on their lips, and to the rich men who subscribe generously to soldiers' and sailors' monument funds, and who ransack ancient chronicles to establish their connection with the heroes of the Revolution. Let the paraders and the ancestor-worshipers unite in a practical recognition of the rights of their belated brothers who are seeking to enter the kingdom of liberty and justice, and they will have given a living shape to the sentiment they symbolically honor, each in his own way.

I am not content if the labor leaders retire from the lobby when all the mills are running full time and shop foremen are scouring the streets for "hands." It is no proof of our sincerity that we are indifferent in times of plenty as to who it is that picks up the crumbs after we have fed. They only are true Americans who, remembering that this country was wrested from the English in the name of the common rights of humanity, resist the temptation to insure their own soup-kettles by patrolling the national pastures and granaries against the hungry from other lands. Share and share alike is the motto of brotherhood.

But who will venture to preach such devotion to principle to the starved and naked and oppressed? Why, I, even I, who refuse to believe that the American workingman is past answering the call of a difficult ideal, no matter what privations are gnawing at his vitals. I have read in the history books that when Lincoln issued his call for volunteers, they came from mills and factories and little shops as promptly as from counting-rooms and college halls. Fathers of large families that looked to him for bread kissed their babies and marched off to the war, taking an elder son or two with them. Were they all aristocrats whose names are preserved on four thousand gravestones at Gettysburg? And who were they who went barefoot in the snow and starved with Washington in Valley Forge? The common people, most of them, the toilers for daily bread, they who give all when they give aught, because they have not enough to divide.

They only mark themselves as calumniators of the poor who protest that times and men have changed since Washington's and Lincoln's day; who think that the breed of heroes died out with the passing of the Yankee farmer and the provincial townsman of the earlier periods. Shall not the testimony of a daughter of the slums be heard when the poor are being judged? I was reared in a tenement district of a New England metropolis, where the poor of many nations contended with each other for a scant living; and the only reason I am no longer of the slums is because a hundred heroes and heroines among my neighbors fought for my release. Not only the members of my family, but mere acquaintances put their little all at my disposal. Merely that a dreamer among them might come to the fulfillment of her dream, they fed and sheltered and nursed me and cheered me on, again and again facing the wolves of want for my sake, giving me the whole cloak if the half did not suffice to save the spark of life in my puny body.

If my knowledge of the slums counts for anything, it counts for a positive assurance that the personal devotion which is daily manifested in the life of the tenements in repeated acts of self-denial, from the sharing of a delicacy with a sick neighbor to the education of a gifted child by the year-long sacrifices of the entire family, is a spark from the smouldering embers of idealism that lie buried in the ashes of sordid existence, and await but the fanning of a great purpose to leap up into a flame of abstract devotion.

Times have changed, indeed, since the days of Washington. His was a time of beginnings, ours is a time ripe for accomplishment. And yet the seed the Fathers sowed we shall not reap, unless we consecrate ourselves to our purpose as they did,—all of us, the whole people, no man presuming to insult his neighbor by exempting him on account of apparent weakness. The common people in Washington's time, and again in Lincoln's time, stood up like men, because they were called as men, not as weaklings who must be coddled and spared the shock of robust moral enterprise. Not a full belly but a brimming soul made heroes out of ploughboys in '76. The common man of to-day is capable of a like transformation if pricked with the electric needle of a lofty appeal. Those who are teaching the American workingman to demand the protection of his job against legitimate alien competition are trampling out the embers of popular idealism, instead of fanning it into a blaze that should transfigure the life of the nation.

A FRESH INFUSION OF PIONEER BLOOD

Idealism of the finest, heroism unsurpassed, are frequently displayed in the familiar episodes of the class war that is going on before our eyes, under unionistic leadership. But it is a narrowing of the vision that makes a great mass of the people adopt as the unit of human salvation the class instead of the nation. The struggle which has for its object the putting of the rapacious rich in their place does not constitute a full programme of national progress. If labor leaders think they are leading in a holy war, they should be the last to encourage disrespect of the principles of righteousness for which they are fighting. It is inconsistent, to put it mildly, to lead a demonstration against entrenched capital on one day, and the next day to head a delegation in Congress in favor of entrenched labor. Is there anything brotherly about a monopolization of the labor market? Substituting the selfishness of the poor for the selfishness of the rich will bring us no nearer the day of universal justice.

Though I should not hesitate to insist on a generous attitude toward the foreigner even if it imposed on our own people all the hardships which are alleged to be the result of immigration, I do not disdain to point out the fact that, when all is said and done, there is enough of America to go around for many a year to come. It is hard to know whether to take the restrictionists seriously when they tell us that the country is becoming overcrowded. The population of the United States is less than three times that of England, and England is only a dot on our map. In Texas alone there is room for the population of the whole world, with a homestead of half an acre for every family of five, and a patch the size of Maryland left over for a public park. A schoolboy's geography will supply the figures for this pretty sum.

The over-supply of labor is another myth of the restrictionist imagination that vanishes at one glance around the country, which shows us crops spoiling for want of harvesters, and women running to the legislature for permission to extend their legal working-day in the fields; such is the scarcity of men. Said ex-Secretary Nagel, commenting upon the immigration bill which was so strenuously pushed by the restrictionists in the Sixty-third Congress, only to be vetoed by President Taft:—

In my judgment no sufficiently earnest and intelligent effort has been made to bring our wants and our supply together, and so far the same forces that give the chief support to this provision of the new bill [a literacy test, intended to check the influx of cheap labor] have stubbornly resisted any effort looking to an intelligent distribution of new immigration to meet the needs of our vast country. [And] no such drastic measure [as the literacy test] should be adopted until we have at least exhausted the possibilities of a rational distribution of these new forces.

Distribution—geographical, seasonal, occupational; that should be our next watch-word, if we are bent on applying our vast resources to our needs. It cannot be too often pointed out that a nation of our political confession is bound to try every other possible solution of her problems before resorting to a measure that encroaches on the rights of humanity. And so far are we from exhausting the possibilities of internal reform that even the most obvious economic errors have not been corrected. It is not good sense nor good morals to keep men at work twelve and thirteen hours a day, seven days in the week, as they do, for example, in the paper-mills. It is bad policy to use women in the mills; it is heinous to use the children. Every one of those over-long jobs should be cut in two; the women should be sent back to the nursery, and the children put to school, and able-bodied men set in their places.

If such a programme, consistently carried out throughout the country, still left considerable numbers unemployed, there is one more remedy we might apply. We might chain to the benches in the city parks, where involuntary idlers now pass the day, all the agents and runners who move around Europe at the expense of steamship companies, labor contractors, and mill-owners. We must *stop* the importation of labor, not talk about stopping it.

To refrain from soliciting immigration is a very different thing from imposing an arbitrary check on voluntary immigration, and gives very different results. The class of men who are lured across the ocean by the golden promises of labor agents are not of the same moral order as those who are spurred to the great adventure by a desire to share in our American civilization. When we restrain the runners, we rid ourselves automatically of the least desirable element of immigration,—the hordes of irresponsible job-hunters without family who do not ask to be steered into the current of American life, and whose mission here is accomplished when they have saved up a petty fortune with which to dazzle the eyes of peasant sweethearts at home. It is this class that contributes, through its ignorance and aloofness, the bulk of the deplorable phenomena which are quoted by restrictionists as arguments against immigration in general. But we must go after them by the direct method, applying the force of the law to the agents who rout them out of their native villages. When we attempt to weed out this one element by indirect methods, such as the oft-proposed literacy test, we are guilty of the folly of discharging a cannon into the midst of the sheepfold with the object of killing the wolf.

If through such a measure as the literacy test the desired results could be insured, we should still be loath to adopt it until every other possible method had been tried. To hit at labor competition through a pretended fear of illiteracy is a tricky policy, and trickery is incompatible with the moral dignity of the American nation. Are we bankrupt in statesmanship that we must pawn the jewel of national righteousness? It required no small amount of ingenuity to find a connection between the immigrant's ability to earn a wage and his inability to read. If the resourceful gentlemen who invented the literacy test would concentrate their talents on the problem of stopping the stimulation of immigration, we should soon hear the last of the over-supply of cheap labor. Where there's a will there's a way, in statecraft as in other things.

It is not enough for the integrity of our principles to scrutinize the ethical nature of proposed legislation. It must be understood in general that whoever asks for restrictive measures as a means of improving American labor conditions must prove beyond a doubt, first, that the evils complained of are not the result of our own sins, and next, that the foreign laborer on coming to America has not exchanged worse conditions for better. The gospel of brotherhood will not let us define our own good in terms of indifference to the good of others.

Preaching selfishness in the name of the American workingman is an insidious way of shutting him out from participation in the national mission. If it is good for the nation to live up to its highest traditions, it cannot be bad for any part of the nation to contribute its share toward the furtherance of the common ideal. For we are not a nation of high and low, where the aristocracy acts and the populace applauds. If America is going to do anything in the world, every man and woman among us will have a share in it.

Objection to the influx of foreign labor is sometimes based on a theory the very opposite of the scarcity of work. Some say that there is altogether too much work being done in this country— that we are developing our natural resources and multiplying industries at a rate too rapid for wholesome growth; and to check this feverish activity it is proposed to cut off the supply of labor which makes it possible.

I doubt, in the first place, if it is reasonable to expect a young nation with half a continent to explore to restrain its activity, as long as there are herculean tasks in sight, any more than we would expect a boy to walk off the diamond in the middle of the game. Or if it is thought best to slacken the speed of material progress, the brakes should be applied at Wall Street, not at Ellis Island. The foreign laborer is merely the tool in the hands of the promoter, indispensable to, but not responsible for, his activities. The workmen come in *after* the promoter has launched his scheme. At least, I have never heard of a development company or industrial corporation organized for the purpose of providing jobs for a shipload of immigrants. That species of philanthropy our benevolent millionaires have not hit on as yet.

It is because the brutal method is the easiest that we are advised to confiscate the tools of industry in order to check the rate of material development. The more dignified way would be to restrain the captains of industry, by asserting our authority over our own citizens in matters affecting the welfare of the nation. An up-to-date mother, desiring that her little boy should not play with the scissors, would be ashamed to put them on a high shelf: she would train the boy not to touch them though they lay within his reach. Why should the assemblage of mothers and fathers who constitute the nation show less pride about their methods than a lone woman in the nursery?

* * * * *

Outside the economic field, fear of the immigrant is perhaps oftenest expressed in the sociological anxiety concerning assimilation. The question is raised whether so many different races, products of a great variety of physical and moral environments, can possibly fuse into a harmonious nation, obedient to one law, devoted to one flag. Some people see no indication of the future in the fact that race-blending has been going on here from the beginning of our history, because the elements we now get are said to differ from us more radically than the elements we assimilated in the past.

To allay our anxiety on this point, we have only to remind ourselves that none of the great nations of Europe that present such a homogeneous front to-day arose from a single stock; and the differences between peoples in the times of the political beginnings of Europe were vastly greater than the differences between East and West, North and South, to-day. Moreover, the European nations were assorted at the point of the sword, while in America the nations are coming together of their own free will; and who can doubt that the spiritual forces of common education, common interests and associations are more effective welding agents than brute force?

Doubts as to the assimilative qualities of current immigration do not exist in the minds of the workers in settlements, libraries, and schools. These people have a faith in the future of the strangers that is based on long and intimate experience with foreigners from many lands. When they are dealing with the normal product of immigration, the people who come here following some dim star of higher destiny for their children, the social missionaries are jubilantly sure of the result; and face to face with the less promising material of the labor camps, where thousands are brought together by the lure of the dollar and are kept together by the devices of economic exploitation, the missionaries are still undaunted. They have discovered that sanitation is a remedy for the filth of the camp; that a spelling-book will make inroads on the ignorance of the mob; that a lecture hall will diminish the business of the saloon and the brothel; that substituting neighborly kindness for brutal neglect will fan to a glow the divine spark in the coarsest natures. And then there is the Goethals way of managing a labor camp.

The remedy for the moral indigestion which unchecked immigration is said to induce is in enlarging the organs of digestion. More evening classes, more civic centers, more missionaries in the field, and above all more neighborly interest on the part of the whole people. If immigration were a green apple that we might take or leave, we might choose between letting the apple alone or eating it and following it up with a dose of our favorite household remedy. But immigration consists of masses of our fellow men moving upon our country in pursuit of their share of human happiness. Where human rights are involved, we have no choice. We have to eat this green apple,—the Law of the Fathers enjoins it on us,—but we have only ourselves to blame if we suffer from colic afterwards, knowing the sure remedy.

There is no lack of resources, material or spiritual, for carrying out our half of the assimilation programme. We have money enough, brains enough, inspiration enough. The only reason the mill is grinding so slowly is that the miller is overworked and the hopper is choked. We are letting a few do the work we should all be helping in. At the settlements, devoted young men and women are struggling with classes that are too large, or turning away scores of eager children, and their fathers and mothers, too, because there are not enough helpers; and between classes they spend their energies in running down subscribers, getting up exhibitions to entice the rich men of the community to come and have a look at their mission and drop something in the plate.

But why should there be a shortage of helpers at the settlement? Have not the rich men sons and daughters, as well as checkbooks? What are those young people doing, dancing the nights away in ballrooms and roof-gardens, season after season, year after year? They should be down on their knees washing the feet of the pilgrims to the shrine of liberty, binding up the wounds of the victims of European despotism, teaching their little foreign brothers and sisters the first steps of civilized life.

Is it preposterous to ask that those who have leisure and wealth should give of these stores when they are needed in the chief enterprise of the nation? In what does patriotism consist if not in helping our country succeed in her particular mission? Our mission—the elevation of humanity—is one in which every citizen should have a share, or he is not an American citizen in the spiritual sense. The poor must give of their little—the workingman must not seek to monopolize the labor market; and the rich must give of their plenty—their time, their culture, their wealth.

Certain texts in the restrictionist teachings are as insulting to our well-to-do citizens as is the labor-monopoly preachment to the classes who struggle for a living. The one assumes that the American workingman puts his family before his country; the other—the cry that we cannot assimilate so many strangers—implies that the country's reservoirs of wealth and learning and unspent energy are monopolized by the well-to-do for their own selfish uses. We know what schools and lectures and neighborhood activities can do to promote assimilation. We cannot fail if we multiply these agencies as fast as the social workers call for them. The means for such extension of service are in the hands of the rich. Whoever doubts our ability to assimilate immigration doubts the devotion of our favored classes to the country's cause.

Upon the rich and the poor alike rests the burden of the fulfillment of the dream of the Fathers, and they are poor patriots who seek to lift that burden from our shoulders instead of teaching us how to bear it nobly. Fresh from the press, there lies on my table, as I write, a review of an important work on immigration, in which the reviewer refers to the "sincere idealists who still cling to the superstition that it is opposition to some predestined divine purpose to suggest the rejection of the 'poor and oppressed.'" It is just such teaching as that, which discards as so much sentimental junk the ideas that made our great men great, that is pushing us inch by inch into the quagmire of materialism. If it is true that our rich care for nothing but their ease, and our poor have no thought beyond their daily needs, it is due to the fact that the canker of selfishness is gnawing at the heart of the nation. The love of self, absorption in the immediate moment, are vices of the flesh which fastened on us during the centuries of our agonized struggle for brute survival. The remedy that God appointed for these evils, the vision of our insignificant selves as a part of a great whole, whose lifetime is commensurate with eternity, the materialists would shatter and throw on the dump of human illusions.

Who talks of superstition in a world built on superstition? Civilization is the triumph of one superstition after another. At the very foundation of our world is the huge superstition of the Fatherhood of God. In a time when the peoples of the earth bowed down to gods of stone, gods of wood, gods of brass and of gold, what more incomprehensible superstition could have been invented than that of an invisible, omnipresent Creator who made and ruled and disciplined the entire universe? One nation ventured to adopt this superstition, and that nation is regarded as the liberator of humanity from the slavery of bestial ignorance. Out of that initial superstition followed, in logical sequence, the superstition of the Brotherhood of Man, spread abroad by a son of the venturesome race; succeeded by a refinement of the same notion, the idea that the Father has no favorite children, but allots to each an equal portion of the goods of His house. That is democracy, the latest superstition of them all, the cornerstone of our Republic, and the model after which all the nations are striving to pattern themselves.

* * * * *

Side by side in our public schools sit the children of many races, ours and others. Week by week, month by month, year by year, the teachers pick out the brightest pupils and fasten the medals of honor on their breasts; and a startling discovery brings a cry to their lips: the children of the foreigners outclass our own! They who begin handicapped, and labor against obstacles, leave our own children far behind on the road to scholarly achievement. In the business world the same strange phenomenon is observed: conditions of life and work that would prostrate our own boys and girls, these others use as a block from which to vault to the back of prancing Fortune. In private enterprises or public, in practical or visionary movements, these outsiders exhibit an intensity of purpose, a passion of devotion that do not mark the normal progress of our own well-cared-for children.

What is the galvanizing force that impels these stranger children to overmaster circumstances and bestride the top of the world? Is there a special virtue in their blood that enables them to sweep over our country and take what they want? It is a special virtue, yes: the virtue of great purpose. The fathers and mothers of these children have not weaned them from the habit of contemplating a Vision. They teach them that, in pursuit of the Vision, bleeding feet do not count. They tell them that many morrows will roll out of the lap of to-day, and they must prepare themselves for a long and arduous march.

That is the reading of the riddle, and if we do not want to be shamed by the newcomers in our midst, we must silence those sophisticated teachers of the people who ridicule or pass over with a smile the idea that we, as a nation, are in pursuit of a Vision, and that those things are good for us which further our quest, and the rest—even to bleeding feet—do not count with us. It is the obliteration of the Vision that causes the emptiness in the lives of our children which they are driven to fill up with tinsel pleasures and meaningless activities of all sorts. The best blood in the world is in their veins,—the blood of heroes and martyrs, of dreamers and doers,—filtered through less than half a dozen generations. If they do not arise and do great deeds all around us, it is because their noble blood is clogged in their veins through the infiltrations of materialism in the teachings of the day.

For such an inconsequential whim as that men should be free to pray in any way they choose, the Pilgrim Fathers betook themselves to a wilderness peopled with savages, preferring to die by the tomahawk rather than submit to clerical authority. The free admission of immigrants is not half so rash an adventure, and the thing to be gained by it is a more obvious good than that of freedom of worship. Even a child can understand that it is better for human beings, be they Russians or Italians or Greeks, to get into a country where there is enough to eat and enough to wear, where nobody is permitted to abuse anybody else, and where story-books are given away, than it is to live in countries where starvation and cruel treatment is the lot of multitudes.

No man worthy of the name will deny that moral paralysis is a worse evil than congestion of the labor market, and moral paralysis creeps on us whenever we throw down the burden of duty to recline in the lap of comfort. We shall see no prodigies in the ranks of our children as long as we are ruled by the calculating commercial spirit which takes nothing on faith, which spurns as impracticable whatever is not easily negotiable, and repudiates our debt to the past as something too fantastic for serious consideration. Before the present era of prosperity set in, a scoffer who would brand as superstition the ideas for which our forefathers died would not have spoken with the expectation of being applauded, as he does to-day. Worldly things, like comfort, position, security, and what is called success, have absorbed our attention to such a degree that some of us have forgotten that there is any good save the good of the flesh. Possessions have crowded out aspirations, the applause of the world has become more necessary than the inner satisfactions, and the whole horizon of life is filled with the glaring bulk of an overwhelming prosperity.

No wonder a prophet like Edward Everett Hale was moved to pray before his assembled congregation, "Deliver us, O Lord! from our terrible prosperity." He saw what the worship of fleshly good did to our children: how it stripped from them the wings of higher ambition, and shackled their feet, that should be marching on to the conquest of spiritual worlds, with the weight of false successes. "Deliver us, O Lord! from our terrible prosperity," that our children may have burdens to lift, that they may learn to clutch at things afar, and their sight grow strong with gazing after visions. "Deliver us, O Lord! from our terrible prosperity," that simplicity of life may strip from us all sophistication, till we learn to honor the dreamers in our midst, and our prophets have a place in the councils of the nation.

* * * * *

Not the good of the flesh, but that of the spirit is the good we seek. If it is good for the soul of this nation that we should walk in the difficult path our Fathers trod, harkening only to the inner voice, never pausing to hear the counsels of cold prudence, then assuredly it is good for us to lift up the burdens of welcoming and caring for our brothers from other lands, thus putting into fuller use the instrument of democracy the Fathers invented,—our

Republic, founded to promote liberty and justice among men.

Or if we despise the omens, refuse to take up the difficult task where our predecessors left off, what awaits us? If we persist in pampering ourselves as favorite children, and bedeck ourselves with prosperity's coat of many colors, how long will it be before the less favored brethren, covetous of our superabundance, will strip us and sell us into the bondage of decadence? Immigration on a large scale into every country as thinly populated as ours must go on, will go on, as long as there are other countries with denser populations and scantier resources for sustaining them. Right through history, the needy peoples have gone in and taken possession of the fat lands of their neighbors. Formerly these invasions were effected by force; nowadays they are largely effected by treaties, laws, international understandings. But always the tide flows from the lands of want to the lands of plenty. Nature is behind this movement; man has no power to check it permanently. We in America may, if we choose, shut ourselves up in the midst of our plenty and gorge till we are suffocated, but that will only postpone the day of a fair division of our country's riches. We shall grow inert from fullness, drunk with the wine of prosperity, and presently some culminating folly, such as every degenerate nation sooner or later commits, will leave us at the mercy of the first comers, and our spoils will be divided among the watchers outside our gates.

These things will not happen in a day, nor in a generation, nor in a century, but have we no care for the days that will follow ours? When we talk about providing for to-morrow, let us, in the name of all the wisdom that science has so laboriously amassed, think of that distant to-morrow when the things we now do will have passed into history, to stand for the children of that time either as a glorious example or a fearful warning. If we settle the immigration question selfishly, we shall surely pay the penalty for selfishness. And the rod will smite not our own shoulders, but the shoulders of countless innocents of our begetting.

The law that the hungry shall feed where there is plenty is not the only one which we defy when we turn away the strangers now at our gates. A narrow immigration policy is in opposition also to a primary law of evolution, the law of continuous development along a given line until a climax is reached. Now the evolution of society has been from small isolated groups to larger intermingling ones. In the beginning of political history, every city was a world unto itself, and labored at its own salvation behind fortified walls that shut out the rest of the world. Presently cities were merged into states, states united into confederacies, confederacies into empires. Peoples at first unknown to each other even by name came to pass in and out of each other's territories, merging their interests, their cultures, their bloods.

This process of the removal of barriers, begun through conquests, commerce, and travels, is approaching completion in our own era, through the influences of science and invention. "The world is my country" is a word in many a mouth to-day. East and West hold hands; North and South salute each other. There remain a few ancient prejudices to overcome, a few stumps of ignorance to uproot, before all the nations of the earth shall forget their boundaries, and move about the surface of the earth as congenial guests at a public feast.

This, indeed, will be the proof of the ancient saying, "He hath made of one blood all nations of men, for to dwell on all the face of the earth." It is coming, inevitably it is coming. We in America are in a position to hasten the climax of the drama of unification. If, instead of hastening it, we seek to delay it, we step aside from the path of the world's progress.

America is not God's last stand. That which is to be is conditioned by what has been. Sometime, somewhere, the Plan that the centuries have brooded over will come perfect out of the shell of Time. I am not afraid that humanity will stop short of its inevitable climax, but I am so jealous for the glory of my country that I long to have America retain the leadership which she has held so nobly for a while. I desire that the mantle of the New England prophets should rest on the shoulders of our own children.

Of the many convincing arguments that have been advanced in support of the proposition that immigration is good for us, I shall quote only one, in the words of Grace Abbott, of Chicago, when she sums up a study of eleven immigrant nationalities from southern and eastern Europe. "It was the faith in America and not the occasional criticism that touched me most," she writes, referring to the sayings of the foreigners. "I felt then, as I have felt many times when I have met some newcomer who has expected a literal fulfillment of our democratic ideals, that fortunately for America we had great numbers who were coming to remind us of the 'promise of American life,' and insisting that it should not be forgotten."

All the rest of the arguments—utilitarian, humanitarian, and scientific—I willingly omit. For I do not want the immigrant to be admitted because he can help us dig ditches and build cities and fight our battles in general. I beg that we make this a question of principle first, and of utility afterwards. Whether immigration is good for us or not, I am very certain that the decadence of idealism is bad for us, and that is what I fear more than the restrictionist fears the immigrant.

It should strengthen us in our resolution to abide by the Law of the Fathers—the law of each for all, and all for each—if we find that the movement of democracy to which they imparted such a powerful impulse appears to be in the direct path of social evolution. But even if such omens were lacking I should still pray for strength to cling to the ideal which is defined in the opening words of the Declaration of Independence. For I perceive that here, in the trial at Ellis Island, we are put to the test of the fiery furnace. It was easy to preach democracy when the privileges we claimed for ourselves no alien hordes sought to divide with us. But to-day, when humanity asks us to render up again that which we took from the English in the name of humanity, do we dare to stand by our confession of faith? Those who honor the golden images of self-interest and materialism threaten us with fearful penalties in case we persist in our championship of universal brotherhood. They are binding our hands and feet with the bonds of selfish human fears. The fiery glow of the furnace is on our faces—and the world holds its breath.

*****

Once the thunders of God were heard on Mount Sinai, and a certain people heard, and the blackness of idolatry was lifted from the world. Again the voice of God, the Father, shook the air above Bunker Hill, and the grip of despotism was loosened from the throat of panting humanity.

Let the children of the later saviors of the world be as faithful as the children of the earlier saviors, and perhaps God will speak again in times to come.

THE END

www.ingramcontent.com/pod-product-compliance
Lightning Source LLC
LaVergne TN
LVHW041549070426
835507LV00011B/1005